DEFYING GRAVITY
Break Free from the Culture of More

Defying Gravity
Break Free from the Culture of More

Defying Gravity: Break Free from the Culture of More
978-1-5018-1340-5
978-1-5018-1341-2 *eBook*

Defying Gravity: Leader Guide
978-1-5018-1342-9
978-1-5018-1343-6 *eBook*

Defying Gravity: DVD
978-1-5018-1344-3

Defying Gravity: Program Tools
978-1-5018-1351-1 *Flash Drive*
978-1-5018-1352-8 *Download*

The Generous Church: A Guide for Pastors
978-1-5018-1349-8
978-1-5018-1350-4 *eBook*

Family Card Pack: 28 Days to the Life You Want
978-1-5018-1353-5

For more information, visit www.AbingdonPress.com.

From Tom Berlin

6 Decisions That Will Change Your Life
6 Ways We Encounter God
6 Things We Should Know About God

From Tom Berlin and Lovett H. Weems, Jr.

Bearing Fruit: Ministry with Real Results
High Yield: Seven Disciplines of the Fruitful Leader
Overflow: Increase Worship Attendance & Bear More Fruit

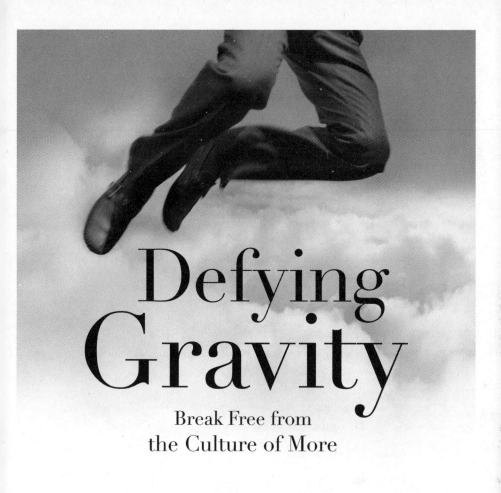

Defying Gravity

Break Free from the Culture of More

TOM BERLIN

Abingdon Press / Nashville

DEFYING GRAVITY
BREAK FREE FROM THE CULTURE OF MORE

This book is printed on elemental chlorine-free paper.

Library of Congress Cataloging-in-Publication data applied for.
978-1-5018-1340-5

16 17 18 19 20 21 22 23 24 25 — 10 9 8 7 6 5 4 3 2 1
MANUFACTURED IN THE UNITED STATES OF AMERICA

To Karen,
the most giving person I know,
whose example led me me to experience
the joy of generosity

CONTENTS

1
DISCOVERING GRAVITY

Happy are those who find wisdom
   and those who gain understanding.
Her profit is better than silver,
   and her gain better than gold.
                    (Proverbs 3:13-14)

1

DISCOVERING GRAVITY

Have you ever felt that you are being pulled by an invisible force, that there is something beyond your rational mind and thinking that directs your behavior? Invisible forces are a part of our world and are at work ordering life as we know it. One such force is gravity.

To understand gravity, you need to meet Isaac Newton. During the summer of 1655 the plague had broken out in European cities, including Cambridge, England. Newton and the other students who attended Cambridge University were sent home for the summer. Newton took his textbooks with him. He believed that God, the ultimate mathematician, periodically whispered secrets into his ears so he could reveal them to the world. We would dismiss

Newton as an egotistical crackpot except for what happened when he locked his door and opened his books that summer.

Newton not only mastered the science of his day but advanced it considerably. He emerged at the end of the summer with new theories that explained everything from light and rainbows to ocean tides. Newton's most startling and perhaps helpful theory was something now known throughout the world as *gravity*.

Gravity is the pull of objects on other objects—the pull of the earth on a rock, for example, to make it fall from your hand when you release it. Newton looked through a relatively new invention called the telescope and was aware that the moon was probably nothing more than a large rock, so why would it act differently? Why didn't it fall to the ground? Newton theorized that the moon is actually falling from the sky toward the earth, but due to its forward motion, it is in what is called *orbit* around the earth. Newton surmised that God put the moon in motion in such a way that it would perpetually and dependably appear in the sky each night, its journey directed by the earth's gravity. Newton helped us understand that a force you cannot see can have great effect on your life and that no one is exempt. Objects as big as the moon are affected by the same force that controls you and me.[1]

Every day, we experience this force that we call gravity; in fact, gravity makes our lives possible. Sandra Magnus, an astronaut who once lived on the international space station, understood exactly how important gravity is to our daily lives after she attempted to cook in space. Imagine, for a moment, what would happen if you cut up an onion without the aid of gravity. The outer peel would go in one direction, and squares of chopped onion would fan out before you, each on its own little space mission. The liquid inside the onion would form tiny drops that would float about the galley. All these particles would threaten the sanitation of the space station as well as its electronic equipment. Magnus overcame these obstacles by using a collection of plastic bags, Velcro, duct tape, and a small paring knife. She attached peels to duct tape on the counter and chopped ingredients inside plastic bags that would corral the pieces until they were added to the dish. A dish that would take minutes on earth required hours in space, all because of the lack of gravity. Right now the perfect amount of gravity orders your world, making everything easier and more dependable.[2]

FINANCIAL GRAVITY

I suggest that just as gravity exists in the natural world, *financial gravity* exists in the economic world where you and I live each day. Like the gravity of our planet, financial gravity enables us to function in our daily lives. It is the invisible force that compels us to pursue our basic necessities—things such as food, shelter, and clothing for ourselves and those we love.

These benefits of financial gravity are important for Christians to remember when thinking about generosity and stewardship, because it is easy to believe that money and possessions are the root of all evil. This is a common misquotation of 1 Timothy 6:10, which states that not money itself, but "the *love* of money is the root of all kinds of evil. Some have wandered away from the faith and have impaled themselves with a lot of pain because they made money their goal" [emphasis added].

The problem with financial gravity occurs when you feel it with such intensity that it changes the way you live your life. You sense it at certain moments, such as when you examine your bank account, noting the balance is lower than you had hoped for, or when you see that your credit card bill is higher than you would like. You feel it when you open up an Internet browser and see ads posted for items that are magically in the styles and colors you like. When you walk down the street of the local town center, with its eclectic mix of retail stores, specialty shops, cinemas, and restaurants, you can almost reach out and touch the force I am describing. Enter a shopping mall, and it is palpable. There is something attempting to pull you inside each store as you pass.

Besides our basic needs, all of us have wants. For most people, the list of wants is never short. Along with items we don't currently have, our wants include things we already have but would like to improve. A newer car, a faster computer, a larger home, a flatter TV, a designer blouse or suit—all these are items that could be found on our want list. The longer the list, the more financial gravity exerts its pull.

When financial gravity is experienced to the extreme, it's like living on Jupiter. Because of the large mass of the planet, a man who weighs a lean 150 pounds on Earth would suddenly weigh over 350 pounds! His once-light steps would require a plodding effort as he drags himself from place to place on Jupiter. Life would become laborious. After a short journey, he wouldn't be sure he could move anymore.

Sometimes we feel weighed down by financial gravity in the same way. When that happens, the bulk of our energy is spent navigating the material world. In extreme cases, we lose our freedom.

THE KINGDOM OF SELF

Jesus recognized the problem of financial gravity and addressed it in his teaching. One day a nice young man came to Jesus with a serious question: "Teacher, what good deed must I do to have eternal life?" (Matthew 19:16 NRSV).

Jesus told the young man to keep the commandments. As Jesus reviewed several specific requirements of the law, you could almost hear the sound of check marks being made in this fellow's mind.

> The young man said to him, "I have kept all these; what do I still lack?" Jesus said to him, "If you wish to be perfect, go, sell your possessions, and give the money to the poor, and you will have treasure in heaven; then come, follow me." When the young man heard this word, he went away grieving, for he had many possessions." (Matthew 19:20-22 NRSV)

Think about what this guy missed. Jesus issued him a once-in-a-lifetime offer, to be the thirteenth disciple. The young man could have heard Jesus teach daily, participated in miracles, and helped form the early church. His name would have gone down in history. But, hearing Jesus' terms, "he went away." You have to ask, *Why on earth would he go away?* The young man obviously was serious about living a godly life. He had worked the spiritual soil of his life, excited about what he would harvest later. He knew

Jesus could help him go deeper. What would make him walk away from all that?

It's important to note the young man's emotional state as he walked away from the opportunity Jesus gave him. Notice that he went away *grieving*. He was sad to leave. Being near Jesus caused him to be pulled in a new direction. Simultaneously, at the thought of liquidating his wealth, he felt financial gravity exert its pull in a way that suddenly was palpable. His emotional response in that moment is a testimony to the confusion and disorientation he felt. The young man was torn between two worlds. He wanted to go with Jesus and learn how to give his life fully to God. He wanted to experience a deeper righteousness. But he could not bear to sell his possessions. He knew he was tearing up the winning ticket in the discipleship lottery, and he wept.

Here is what Jesus told his disciples about the young man's decision: "Truly I tell you, it will be hard for a rich person to enter the kingdom of heaven. Again I tell you, it is easier for a camel to go through the eye of a needle than for someone who is rich to enter the kingdom of God" (Matthew 19:23-24 NRSV).

Jesus was making an important observation to his disciples: There are two worlds where we can live, the kingdom of self and the kingdom of God. The kingdom of self is the world we see and touch every day. It is the world lived from the perspective of self. It is where we disproportionately feel financial gravity.

Like you, I live in a little kingdom. It is called the kingdom of Tom. I don't like to admit it, but in this kingdom I work hard to order life the way I want. I choose my friends. I try to influence people and situations to go the way I think is best.

Once on a trip to Sierra Leone, Africa, I visited the capital city, Freetown, and stayed in an area called *Kingtom*. No kidding. They had a large billboard with *Kingtom* written on it. I had to beat back tall brush so I could have my picture taken in front of it, and it was completely worth the effort. There I stood with my royal name emblazoned in a bold, billboard-sized font. When I got home, I showed the picture to everyone and told them I had found my place in the world. My family suggested that it was a place far, far away.

You have a little kingdom too. It's the world you have created that includes your family and friends, work, and hobbies, your home and possessions, your abilities and interests. You manage this world. You are the king or queen of this domain. In his book, *The Divine Conspiracy*, Dallas Willard writes, "Our 'kingdom' is simply the range of our effective will. Whatever we genuinely have the say over is in our kingdom. And our having the say over something is precisely what places it within our kingdom."[3]

Willard's reminder about the confines of our kingdom is helpful. God has made us to enjoy life and have influence in the world. The problem is that we lose perspective. We often think that *our* world is *the* world. Most of us protect the boundaries of our realm fiercely. We pull up the drawbridge when other people try to impose their opinions or attempt to alter our domain. The reason is that in our kingdom, as in any kingdom, the royals are innately self-interested. We do not want to lose the power or trappings of our reign.

This may explain the force that pulls us in many areas of life. When we're hesitant to aid a fellow motorist whose car is on the side of the road with a flat tire, it's often because we sense that the act of kindness will cost us too much time or effort. The king (or queen) has other more pressing business that day. We struggle to listen to a friend as she shares the trouble her child is having in school, and rather than focus on what's being said, we check the time. We think about the messages on our phone and all that needs to be accomplished that afternoon. It's impossible to serve our friend and these demands at the same time. In both cases, we're pulled back into our own little world rather than serving the needs that have been presented to us.

The kingdom of self operates now in much the same way it did in biblical times. Though our technology and civilization have progressed considerably, the human condition has not. Most of the opportunities and hardships people experienced in those days are still with us. People still struggle with selfishness and commit the same sins. The reason is that, while we may be located on planet Earth, we are actually living in our own little worlds.

This was the dilemma of the rich young man. He was grieving because Jesus, in asking him to sell his possessions, was suggesting that the young man dismantle his world to join Jesus in a different one. In the kingdom of self, the pull of financial gravity was simply too great for the young man to overcome.

THE KINGDOM OF GOD

As the rich young man walked away, Jesus shared good news with his disciples: There was another world they could enter. It was called the kingdom of God, and it was breaking into a world full of fiefdoms. This announcement of God's kingdom was a regular part of Jesus' teaching. "The time has come," he said. "The kingdom of God has come near. Repent and believe the good news!" (Mark 1:15 NIV).

The message of this alternative kingdom was urgent to Jesus. No matter where he traveled, he told people he could not stay with them for very long. He kept on the move from village to village, town to town. "But he said to them, "I must preach the good news of God's kingdom in other cities too, for this is why I was sent" (Luke 4:43).

Jesus came not only to tell us that God's kingdom is present in the world but that we can fully enter and participate in it. This is the good news, that we can abundantly experience God's kingdom, and that its goodness can be our own. Jesus told parables so that people would understand what the kingdom of God is like. He had to explain the properties and forces of God's kingdom, because they are so different from those present in the kingdom of self.

In the kingdom of self, people often end up wounded; but Jesus taught and demonstrated that when people are present in the kingdom of God, they are healed. In the kingdom of self, grudges prevail; but in the kingdom of God, people are forgiven of sins. In the kingdom of self, envy, strife, contempt, and bitterness abide, but in the kingdom of God, kindness, compassion, love, and justice reign.

It has been the Lord's intention from the beginning of creation that we live in the kingdom of God. Jesus is the force that leads us there.

DEFYING GRAVITY

Of course, *follow me* is a simple and open invitation, but doing so can be difficult. The forces we experience in the kingdom of self hold us down and keep us from a better way of life. The gravity of our lives, especially when unexamined, can be oppressive. To experience the kingdom of God, we must defy gravity, let go, and truly submit to Christ.

Dallas Willard provides a helpful description of what happens when we defy gravity.

> By relying on his word and presence we are enabled to reintegrate the little realm that makes up our life into the infinite rule of God....Caught up in his active rule, our deeds become an element in God's eternal history. They are what God and we do together, making us part of his life and him a part of ours.[4]

Make no mistake, the values and practices of the kingdom of God are not intuitive to most people. We have lived in our own worlds so long that what Jesus describes may feel abnormal and even objectionable. Just think about some of the values Jesus taught:

Humility

"Whoever wants to be first among you will be the slave of all." (Mark 10:44)

Trust

"Therefore, don't worry and say, 'What are we going to eat?' or 'What are we going to drink?' or 'What are we going to wear?'

Gentiles long for all these things. Your heavenly Father knows that you need them. Instead, desire first and foremost God's kingdom and God's righteousness, and all these things will be given to you as well." (Matthew 6:31-33)

Forgiveness

"Don't judge, and you won't be judged. Don't condemn, and you won't be condemned. Forgive, and you will be forgiven." (Luke 6:37)

Sacrifice

"Those who love their lives will lose them, and those who hate their lives in this world will keep them forever." (John 12:25)

The forces and assumptions of our world are often polar opposites of those in the kingdom of God that Jesus proclaimed. That's why, in order to enter that kingdom, we must accept Jesus as the new gravitational center of our lives.

WHAT IS IT ABOUT MONEY?

In the story of the rich young man, notice that Jesus didn't just offer a choice between the kingdom of self and the kingdom of God. He went beyond that to draw a connection between wealth and the difficulty of leading a godly life: "Truly I tell you, it will be hard for a rich person to enter the kingdom of heaven" (Matthew 19:23 NRSV).

This may seem a bit unfair (especially if you are rich). Most scholars believe that Jesus, in talking about a camel and the eye of a needle, was using an extreme metaphor to make a point. That point was brought home dramatically on a recent trip to the Holy Land, when our guide took us to a small "Needle Gate" in the basement of a Russian Orthodox church in Jerusalem's Old City. The guide suggested that this secondary gate had been created intentionally small so that invaders could not easily pass through when the main gate was closed. A camel, for instance, would have to get on its knees and crawl through the opening. Whether a metaphor or a real gate into the city, the lesson is the same: There is something about the pull of wealth that can work against the pull of a godly life.

Notice that Jesus said it was *hard* for a rich person to enter the kingdom of heaven, but he didn't say it was *impossible*. When I was a young pastor, I lived under the false impression that, deep down, wealthy people were probably not godly people. I had formed a stereotype based on movies and novels that portrayed wealthy people as shallow, self-serving, and greedy. I could hold that opinion for two reasons. First, I didn't understand that I was wealthy compared to much of the world's population. God found some vivid ways to open my eyes on this point. Second, I didn't actually know any people of substantial wealth. However, I've found that one of the things God likes to do when I judge others unfairly is lead me to relationships in which I get to know people and discover I am wrong.

Over the years, as I encountered people of wealth, I discovered that my stereotype was not only unfair but the opposite was often true. One reason for this unexpected finding was the very thing we've been discussing: financial gravity. Gravity pulls all matter together; the more matter, the more gravity. For example, the sun has such a huge mass that it can hold the entire solar system together. Similarly, money and possessions have mass; they pull us in. The more we amass, the more we experience that pull. I've found, as a result, that wealthy people who are Christians are often the most disciplined about doing good works. It's because they have to be. They understand that if they don't manage their money, it soon will control them.

In my experience, Christians who have greater affluence often think far more about the role of wealth in their discipleship. Those who own businesses may have deep concern about the health of their companies, knowing that their employees and their families depend on its success for their livelihoods. Most of them understand that prosperity is connected to the performance of those who work for them, so they offer fair salaries and benefits to retain workers and demonstrate their appreciation. In private moments, these people often struggle with the question of whether they are honoring God fully with their wealth. They ponder seriously this Bible passage: "From everyone to whom much has been given, much will be required; and from the one to whom much has been entrusted, even more will be demanded" (Luke 12:48 NRSV).

Most of us, wealthy or not, resonate with the truth of what Jesus observed when he said it's hard for a rich person to enter the kingdom of heaven. So, what is it about the gravitational pull of money and wealth that can easily take our focus away from faith in God? It's hard to say, but I feel it.

Recently I went into a large electronics store to buy a mobile phone charger. Now, I am on the road of transformation and have the power of Jesus in my life, and yet I found it nearly impossible to walk straight to the mobile phone department, because on the way I went through the washer and dryer section. Our washer and dryer are in great shape, but the new stainless steel, top-loading machines looked like something out of a space movie, and they were calling to me. From there I followed the path to the land of a thousand TVs. It was a magical place where the same basketball game was playing on each screen. Banks of monitors covered the back wall of the store, and as I slowly walked by, I tried to see the subtle differences among them as the price tags got higher and higher. Passing the island of surround sound, I crossed into the peninsula of computers and peripherals. I tried on a headset I didn't need, just to see if it was as comfortable as advertised. I compared brands and prices. I noted memory capacities and screen sizes. I meandered into the software section and looked at things that could improve my efficiency and entertain me for hours. Then I saw the time and realized I would soon be late to pick up my daughter. Looking up, surrounded on all sides by wonderful devices, I had just one question: What had I come to purchase in the first place? It took me a good five minutes to remember.

24

IS THIS YOU?

This is the power of possessions and the "pull" that financial gravity can have on our lives. To resist that pull, we need to make plans and develop habits that will help us stop being collectors of goods and become stewards who participate in the creation of God's kingdom.

An important part of stewardship is giving, and sometimes we are reluctant to give. Our reluctance to give money is based on the many effects of financial gravity, all which have to do with the upkeep of the kingdom of self. Let me share some profiles that may help you identify your own reluctance about giving.

Batten Down the Hatches

This person feels great anxiety about money no matter what the circumstance. Normal life experiences that require financial planning—such as helping a child go to college, saving for a special vacation, or preparing for retirement—are experienced as coming economic hurricanes that are gaining strength on open waters before they make landfall. This person is hyper-focused on saving and feels such urgency that often it's difficult for the person to spend money on himself or herself, much less give it away.

Every Rung Goes Higher and Higher

When we climb our way to a certain lifestyle, it requires all the household income just to sustain our standard of living. When our income increases, rather than pay off a credit card or give to the church, we use the extra money to move up another rung on the ladder. We remodel the house, purchase a new fishing boat, or trade up for a nicer model car. With each new rung, we feel the need for more possessions and a higher standard of living in retirement. Giving is postponed indefinitely, to be done one day when the bills are finally paid.

The Call of the Wild

For some people, a simple trip to the local superstore for a few groceries can become a safari deep into the thicket of the retail jungle. Big game items in the electronics department call the hunter to mount them on the wall. Sale signs mark the trail. A pause in the clothing section makes one think, I would look great in that fedora. I've never owned a fedora. Today I will fulfill that destiny! The shopping adventure is satisfying until the bills come due. Our inability to control spending when faced with the allure of merchandise means that other financial priorities suffer.

I Am the Gift

Those of us in human service fields, such as teachers, pastors, social workers, and employees at nonprofits, often have lower salaries and spend our time and talent each day assisting others who often are in difficult social situations. We can fall into the trap of thinking, My whole day was a gift. Soon that becomes a reason for neglecting financial giving.

Bucket List Bingo

Some people take the concept of a bucket list very seriously. They have a strong sense that life is finite and that the day is coming when we won't be able to have the experiences we might enjoy today. When an e-mail offers a trip to an exotic location, it can be nearly irresistible. When friends talk about an experience that will be expensive, but then add that you only live once, they feel compelled to sign up. Bucket listers live for big-ticket adventures, and their discretionary income is used to make checks on the list.

Each of these profiles involves something of merit. Saving for the future is essential. Creating a lifestyle that works for us is a good thing. Travel is a way to understand and appreciate the world and its cultures. Great experiences bring us closer to family and friends. However, each profile, under financial stress, yields a similar result: There's nothing left to give. Generosity is simply not possible.

Do you have a problem with financial gravity? Maybe scanning these profiles and understanding your financial motivations will help you answer that question. Then, when Jesus invites us to give our lives to the work of God's kingdom, we can better understand both the insight that brought the young man to Jesus and his sorrow when he walked away.

Jesus understands these dynamics and the choices that are involved, as we can tell from his conversation with the young man. Jesus challenged the young man to defy financial gravity, and the young man turned away. For him, and for many of us, defying gravity is that one thing needed to accomplish the goal of loving God completely.

The good news is that Jesus offers us a way to enter the gravitational field of God's kingdom. Just as money and possessions can weigh us down, they also can be a part of what sets us free.

2

BREAKING FREE

Tell them to do good, to be rich in the good things they do, to be generous, and to share with others.

(1 Timothy 6:18)

2

BREAKING FREE

There is another rich young man who appears in the gospels. This young man is a character in a parable Jesus told about a loving father. He is the younger of two sons, and he feels the force of financial gravity so strongly that he goes to his father and asks for his inheritance.

Even today this would be quite a request. I'm trying to imagine how the conversation would go if I went to my father, who turned eighty this year, and asked for some portion of his property. I can think of several words to describe how he might react: *flabbergasted, flummoxed*. Maybe somewhere between *disconcerted* and *blown away*. To ask for an inheritance early is the equivalent of saying that you've grown impatient for your parent's death. *You've lived a good long life, Pop—frankly, a little too long. I'd like to get the cash before you blow it all on a nice trip or on care for yourself and mom in your golden years.* I can also think of a word my brothers might use to describe my status in the family after such a request: *banished.*

That's what would happen today. In the first-century culture of Israel, such a request would be so offensive that there probably are no words to capture adequately the family's reaction to the younger son's wish. The anger would be as high as the hurt would be deep.

Parables often place people in peculiar scenarios to make their point clear. This young man wants to leave his father's home to pursue the kingdom of self. He walks out the door with more money than he has ever possessed in his young life. He must feel light and free as he sets his course and begins to experience the pull of a distant land. Having spent his life in a fairly confined space, he is excited to begin a great adventure. What he doesn't know is that he is about to be sucked into a black hole.

BLACK HOLES

A *black hole* is a location in space where the gravity is so great that nothing can escape its pull, even light, which is why black holes can be felt but not seen. Astronomers know a black hole is there because of the way its extreme gravity affects the stars, gas, and planets around it. Once something enters the gravitational field of a black hole, the effect is dramatic.

From time to time, my wife Karen reminds me of a vacation in which I was physically present but emotionally absent because I fell deep into an espionage novel. When she hinted it was time for dinner, I tried to make her understand that the fate of the world was at stake. If I stopped reading, there was no telling what might happen to the main character. When she suggested we take a long hike, I suggested a shorter route, knowing that if I didn't get back to that novel, sinister agents might detonate a nuclear bomb. I felt like pleading, Do you know what's at stake here?

I had fallen so deep into that book that one night I sneaked out of bed, went to another room, and started reading by headlamp. When I looked up, I saw that Karen had entered the room, as stealthy as a character in my book. She said, "I know what you're doing, and I'm okay with it because we're on vacation. But why don't you stay up and finish the book so that tomorrow we can have a nice day?"

That's the thing about black holes. Once you fall into one, it is hard to think about anyone or anything else. And the kingdom of self is full of black holes.

Money and the things it buys can produce a field of gravity so strong that many people simply cannot escape, especially those with low spiritual and emotional maturity. One such person is the young man in Jesus' parable. His spending choices are predictable and quickly summarized: "Soon afterward, the younger son gathered everything together and took a trip to a land far away. There, he wasted his wealth through extravagant living" (Luke 15:13).

Most of us understand the problem faced by the young man. He is anxious to be independent. The immaturity that limited his vision to a brief few hours into the future is surpassed only by an impulse control so weak that all options for spending Daddy's money looked equally inviting. He lives fast and large until it's all gone, then stumbles in regret when a famine picks the last denarius from his pocket.

Few of us have done anything as extreme and irresponsible as this young man, and yet there are elements of his story that seem common to us all. Financial abundance carries the promise of stability and a blessed future but can lead to disaster. A large sum of money looks like a granite boulder that will endure time, until we discover that it's more like sand on a barrier island that can be washed away overnight by tides or a nor'easter. The young man in Jesus' parable is on a journey where eventually he will discover that the key to a good life can be found in a quality he has been least likely to possess: generosity.

GENEROSITY

Christian Smith and Hilary Davidson's book *The Paradox of Generosity* shares data captured in Smith's five-year, multi-disciplinary Science of Generosity initiative. Its survey of two thousand Americans, along with in-depth interviews, offers new insights into the outcomes of generosity when exhibited or withheld in the life of an individual or family. Smith and Davidson define generosity as "the virtue of giving good things to others freely and abundantly."

This was not always the definition. The word *generosity* derives from the Latin word *generōsus,* which was used to denote a person of noble birth. Up to and including the sixteenth century, when the word *generous* was used in English it meant that a person was born into aristocracy. It described a person of noble lineage whose family was probably one of influence and wealth. It was meant for an elite class of people who had special resources at their disposal. The word did not necessarily mean that those people used their resources for any other purpose than to support their own lifestyle. However, it may be one reason why people today sometimes think that generosity, especially financial generosity, is the responsibility of those who have great wealth and not something that the average person should think about or practice. This thinking is consistent with the original use of the word.

Thankfully the use of the word *generous* changed over time. It evolved from a descriptor of the status into which you were born to the character you possessed. By the seventeenth century, to be generous meant to possess a noble spirit. It meant that certain character traits such as gallantry, courage, strength, gentleness, and fairness were evidenced in a person's life. The word continued to change in meaning through the eighteenth and nineteenth centuries, in ways that are more similar to its current usage. Today *generous* describes a person who is altruistic, who sees the needs of others and takes steps to meet those needs.[1]

Interestingly, both the original and current meanings of the word reflect critical elements of our faith in Christ. We find the original meaning when Paul tells us in his letters (Romans 8:15; Ephesians 1:5) that through Christ we have been adopted into the family of God; we are members of a noble family. The author of First John captures the same idea when he writes, "See what kind of love the Father has given to us in that we should be called God's children, and that is what we are!" (1 John 3:1).

The current meaning of the word *generous* applies to Christians as well. We are called to grow in the love of Christ in such a way that, while enjoying the privilege of membership in a noble family, we learn to possess a noble spirit. Paul writes in Philippians 2:

> Do nothing from selfish ambition or conceit, but in humility regard others as better than yourselves. Let each of you look not to your own interests, but to the interests of others. Let the same mind be in you that was in Christ Jesus,
>
> > who, though he was in the form of God,
> > > did not regard equality with God
> > > as something to be exploited,
> > but emptied himself,
> > > taking the form of a slave,
> > > being born in human likeness.
> > And being found in human form,
> > > he humbled himself
> > > and became obedient to the point of death—
> > > even death on a cross. (Philippians 2:3-8 NRSV)

Paul calls us to adopt the personal qualities and outlook on life that Jesus possessed. Jesus was of the noblest stock. He was the very nature of God. Yet, Jesus humbled himself and displayed his nobility by generously taking on the form of a human. Not only did he become a man but he died on a cross, the worst form of death imaginable. Jesus offered his life for the lives of many. On the cross we see the goodness of his ultimate act of generosity. In his resurrection we see the nobility of his being, which cannot be diminished by death. Christ's offer of salvation in his death and resurrection is his way of meeting prodigals like us on the road, forgiving our sins, and restoring the image of God within us.

OUR CHALLENGE

Paul challenges us to respond to God's loving initiative. We are called to abandon the lesser habits and behaviors of a world influenced by sin and allow ourselves to be transformed by the noble character of Christ, which is known by its generosity: "Let the same mind be in you that was in Christ Jesus...."

To live the Christian life, then, is to enter into the way of Christ in such a manner that the forces of God's kingdom begin to order our actions and thoughts. Paul understands that in order to experience this transformation, we will have to defy the gravitational forces and black holes of the kingdom of self and allow Christ to pull us into a new reality. Such a change will primarily be the work of the Holy Spirit in our lives, but it also requires a response from us to the Spirit's initiative.

In First Thessalonians, Paul writes, "We appealed to you, encouraged you, and pleaded with you to live lives worthy of the God who is calling you into his own kingdom and glory" (1 Thessalonians 2:12). Paul says that the movement from the kingdom of self to the kingdom of God is the greatest gravity-defying moment of life. It is the ultimate experience of freedom: "Christ has set us free for freedom. Therefore, stand firm and don't submit to the bondage of slavery again" (Galatians 5:1).

Paul tells us that within this freedom, we will no longer be ruled by the self-serving inclinations that were normative in our lives before we knew Christ. Instead, we will begin to express noble character traits, including generosity. "By contrast, the fruit of the Spirit is love, joy, peace, patience, kindness, generosity, faithfulness, gentleness, and self-control" (Galatians 5:22-23 NRSV).

The once-rich but then very poor young man in Jesus' parable eventually returned home. He knew he had squandered his birthright and deserved his father's wrath, but he was malnourished and desperate, so he decided to ask his dad for a job on the estate. As he walked up the familiar road home, he was amazed when he saw the old man running toward him. It was beneath the dignity of older men in Israel to run anywhere, much less toward a son who had brought shame to the family. The son must have taken this as a sign of bad things to come: *Wow, he must be REALLY angry if he is running toward me.* Self-defense may have occurred to him; it is certain that his father's grace did not.

That was the day the son learned of his father's generous spirit. His father joyfully restored him to the household. It was kindness he did not deserve, forgiveness he did not merit, and love he did not anticipate.

Think for a moment how such an experience could have shaped the son's character. What happened that day must have changed the way he saw the world. We can imagine that, from that day forward, he would have been focused on the needs of others more than on himself. The promise of a better life through extravagant living would no longer appeal to him. The joy of extending love and grace to others would motivate his words, thoughts, and actions.

He would listen appreciatively when his father spoke. He would be free of contempt when others made mistakes. He would accept his elder brother's bitterness with self-awareness and humility, since patience itself is an act of generosity.

We can imagine that the pull of self-focus and self-will ceased to have any significant effect on his life. The world outside his parents' circle no longer seemed preferable. Since the day he reentered the gates of his family estate, he was certain that their world was better than the one he had just escaped. Most important of all, rather than simply being a recipient of his father's generosity, he now possessed the insight to become a participant in it.

Just as the pull of financial gravity was evident in the prodigal's life, so we can see it in our own. Consider your prayer life. Often, our prayers to God are about things we hope to receive. We ask for guidance to make decisions, health and recovery from illness, comfort for the bereaved, jobs and money to pay bills, healing in relationships, along with countless other requests. We offer God an extensive to-do list. Our desire, regardless of how well intended, is often related to what we can acquire or receive from God, rather than what we can give. I wonder to what proportion— as individuals, small groups, or churches—we ask God to direct us to reach those who do not know Christ, feed the hungry, comfort those who mourn or exhibit mental illness, house the homeless, gain access to prisoners, or provide needed services such as job training. From my observation, the ratio of "receive" prayers to "serve" prayers is often rather high.

There is a moment of epiphany for Christ followers when we recognize the difference between wanting to be a beneficiary of God's kingdom and wanting to participate in its expansion. Participants want to do what God is doing. When they read Jesus' words in the Bible, they do not see commandments to be begrudgingly kept; they see entranceways into a new life. Christians who long to be participants in God's kingdom have a faith that is significant and an eagerness to depend on God deeply. Churches that want to join Christ in his ministry are communities of vitality.

BECOMING A STEWARD

This orientation toward God's kingdom is life-altering. It creates an identity founded in generosity. Generous people see themselves, their lives, and their purposes differently than people who are weighed down by financial gravity. Generous people are more interested in what they can give than in what they will get. The word that best describes a generous person is *steward*.

A steward is someone who manages another's property or financial affairs. Stewards have broad discretionary powers over how an account is managed or how a household is run, but they understand that they are primarily servants, looking not to self-interest but to the welfare of the owner. Christ followers understand that they are stewards of a precious gift given to them by God—the gift of a life with unique strengths, talents, abilities, and resources to use in ways guided by God's own Spirit.

I learned what it meant to be a steward when I turned fifty. I dreaded my fiftieth birthday because I felt old. I shared my unhappiness about it at church one Sunday. I'm sure what came out of my mouth was something hopeful about how we should thank God for every season of life and a joke about how I was grateful for the promise of the resurrection as I passed my middle age. But inside my head I was feeling grumpy that I could actually be fifty years old, an age I had seen in others but somehow never had thought I would reach myself.

It turns out that you can't cover up grumpy. It leaks out of your pores, and people can spot it a mile away. A woman who must have been about sixty came up to me after the service and tried to console me. She said that turning fifty was nothing, that I wasn't even middle-aged yet. Maybe it was the birthday blues, but in a clearly unpastoral moment I told her, "Thanks for that perspective. But if you double fifty you get a hundred, and no one in my family has lived to a hundred. That means at fifty I'm probably at least half dead." As she walked away I could see she was doing some disturbing mental math.

Let's just say that I needed a good distraction. Then it came. An e-mail announced that in honor of my birthday, I had received the most unusual gift of my life. Some good friends were giving me a large sum to use any way that I wanted. You will be pleased to know that this e-mail was not from Barrister Frank N. Stein from some exotic location with a request to help recover a large sum of money from the estate of a deceased client. The e-mail did not instruct me to send my bank account number and password.

No, these were real people, real friends, who were giving me real money. The gift came with only two conditions. I had to give all the money away, and I had to do so in a period of two months.

At first glance, that would seem to be a simple task. Most people have organizations they admire, people they want to assist, and problems they'd like to help solve. How long could it possibly take to disperse a sum of money, no matter how large?

I sat down and made a list of ways the money could be used. By my standards it was a lot of money, so initially my list was rather long. I realized that it was too long, so I threw it away. Then I did nothing. I did nothing for a few weeks. This surprised me. When I first learned of the gift, I saw myself handing out cash the way John D. Rockefeller used to pass out dimes to kids on the street. I thought about how much fun it would be to bless worthy organizations. I knew I would give a portion of the funds to the church I serve, and I knew personally how that would benefit our ministry. Yet I did nothing. I found a hundred reasons to put off the decision. Rather than refine my list, I sharpened pencils. I found a pen. Should the paper be lined or unlined? I considered the possible benefits of typing the list. I checked the time. I got something to eat. Every time I returned to the task I would sit, stare at the vast white desert stretching for miles across the surface of that paper, and do nothing. My excitement had turned to paralysis.

The clock was running, however, and I knew I needed to disburse the funds. It occurred to me that a starting point would be to write the sum of money at the top of the page. I did that. Then I stared at it for a long time. Looking at the figure, I discovered the reason for my reluctance: it wasn't my money. Giving the money away wasn't just about making me happy; I wanted to please the owner as well. I wanted to do things that were of interest to me—after all, I was the birthday boy—but I also wanted to give to organizations and causes that were of interest to the true owners of the funds. In short, I was a steward.

Realizing I was a steward suddenly made generosity more than an act of kindness; it was an important responsibility. Even though my friends had made no stipulations about who should receive the funds, I wanted to do something that would not only interest me but also please them. I felt truly honored that they would entrust me with this once-in-a-lifetime opportunity. In return, I wanted to honor them in the way the money would be invested.

Using this criterion of common interest between steward and owner, I began to make my list again. Then another thought occurred to me. I recalled the words of a friend who says that it is good to do good, but it is better to do good well. I realized that I not only wanted to give the money away but I also wanted to multiply it. I began to think about ways I could motivate others to be generous as well. I called the executive director of a nonprofit that I knew was struggling to fund a project. I told her I could arrange for a donation to her project if she could find donors who would match the contribution. I did this not only to help her reach her goal but because I knew that my friends would love hearing that their money had been multiplied. In fact, with three separate donations I was able to arrange for matching contributions, so that, in effect, most of the money my friends had contributed was doubled.

Soon I found my initial excitement restored and increased. It was a pleasure to contact those who had given me this amazing birthday gift and share my plans for their money. They were joyful about the causes the money would support and the way others were being motivated to be generous, which made me all the happier. We talked about our mutual interest in generosity and why the things their funds had supported were causes that Karen and I gave to each year. Being a steward drew me closer to these friends and turned my birthday thoughts from death to life.

You can have that same experience anytime you want to. It was through a gift that I learned what it means to be a steward, but the concept can be applied to wealth you already possess. Since we are citizens of God's kingdom, everything we have is from the Creator who gave us our talents, intellect, and abilities. We learn to take on the identity of a steward, asking what would please the owner of our resources.

This is hard to do. The world's gravity pulls us toward a deep belief that we are the sole owners of our possessions. As owners, we use the money we earn to support the lifestyle we desire. We make decisions free of the control and even the consideration of others. Many people think they are not financially generous because they lack the resources. In fact, though, the issue isn't wealth but identity. If we see ourselves as stewards, we understand that we are custodians, not owners, of our possessions. We manage our money and assets with the thought of pleasing the true owner. As stewards, we don't view the world through a quantitative lens showing how much is available but through a qualitative lens showing what can be done with the things God has given us.

STEWARDS OF MORE THAN MONEY

Chee-Yun, one of the notable violinists in the world today, plays a violin built in 1669 by Francesco Ruggieri in Italy. It's an

44

old violin, but when she bought the instrument, it still looked practically new, and even had the original varnish. As a musician, Chee-Yun loves to play for an audience and share her instrument with them. She says:

> I really want to bring the audience into my world of imagination. When the music is exciting, I want them to be on the edge of their seats. When it's beautiful, I want them to sit back and think of their life and the beautiful moments they've had. Sometimes, the music is really fast like a bumblebee and sometimes it's like wind blowing and sometimes it's so sad and sometimes it's like flying through the wilderness on a beautiful day.[2]

Clearly, Chee-Yun is a steward of her violin's beauty and its music. While performing a concert in Israel, she learned more about her violin's unique history from a man in the audience, whose father was familiar with the violin. The man said, "Did you know that one of the previous owners loved [the violin] so much that it was his wish to be buried with it when he passed away?" It seemed the violin had joined its past owner in his crypt for over two hundred years.[3] No wonder the violin had been well-preserved! We can imagine the man lying in his casket, with the violin and bow clutched to his chest. He had defied the old adage, "You can't take it with you." Apparently, if your treasure is the size of a violin or smaller, you can.

Think of the difference between Chee-Yun and the previous owner. Chee-Yun values the instrument so much that she travels the world, sharing its music with as many people as she can. The past owner also knew the value of the great gift in his possession, but rather than being a steward, he chose to keep it for himself, even when he was no longer himself. I wasn't able to find out how the violin was resurrected, but I am sure it's in good hands today. When Chee-Yun plays the instrument, the music soars, fills the air, and blesses everyone who hears it.

How many people die with almost everything they had in life—abilities, talents, resources—having either gone through their fingers or still held tightly in their hands, having served only them? The desire of those who live in God's kingdom is to use the time and treasure of life in ways that honor the giver and bless others. The music of their existence is still in the air decades after their death.

The great part about being a steward is that you can begin at any age. Our daughter Sarah learned about stewardship through baking. She baked cakes, added her secret ingredients, rolled them into balls, and dipped them in chocolate. She was exacting in her proportions and learned to apply the outer coating of chocolate like a skilled confectioner. Each one was like a little work of art. When people ate Sarah's cake balls, they found themselves transported to a happy place where all was well. Visually, they often went through several phases. First they registered surprise. Then they showed deep happiness. While taking the final bite, they took on the anxious look of a person waving goodbye to a dear friend.

Initially, ten-year-old Sarah made and gave cake balls as gifts. One recipient suggested they were so good that she should start a business. This may have been meant simply as a compliment, but Sarah took the suggestion to heart and launched her own business at age eleven. A family friend, hoping to encourage an entrepreneurial young girl, gave Sarah an envelope. Inside was money, along with a note explaining that the funds were intended as start-up capital. Sarah was off to the store to buy gift boxes and drizzle tools. Before we knew it, she had a business card advertising *Sarah B Productions.* Her name appeared in the bottom corner above the title *Chief Executive Officer.*

Sarah began by selling her confections on Valentine's Day and other holidays. Soon orders came to her for baby showers and even a wedding reception. We smiled, thinking it was a nice hobby for an elementary school student. Then the orders continued, and cake balls overran our kitchen during the high school graduation party season. Ingredients were mixed and rolled on the kitchen table. Cakes were baked in the oven. Chocolate was melted on the stove. The finished products were placed in brightly colored wrappers inside clear-top candy boxes. As the orders rolled out, the cash rolled in. It was not long until Sarah was…wait for it… *rolling in the dough.*

Pretty soon, Sarah had enough money that she began to think about what to do with it. She wanted to save most of it. She had a few items she wanted to buy. Then we talked about giving. Karen told her about tithing. I suggested that Sarah might think about giving some of it to the church or another worthy cause.

Sarah considered the matter for a few days and then came to me to ask questions about Mercy Hospital, a medical facility our church sponsors in Sierra Leone, Africa, whose work she learned about from our good friend Dr. Cynthia Horner. I told Sarah that the focus of the hospital's work is maternal and children's health. Many women die in childbirth in Sierra Leone due to lack of medical facilities, and the mortality rate of children under the age of five is one of the highest in the world. Sarah told me to wait a minute and went upstairs. She reappeared a few minutes later with a stack of bills totaling over two hundred dollars. "Dad," she said, "can you give this to Dr. Horner for me to take to Mercy when she goes to Sierra Leone? And please, tell that lady I said to keep up the good work!"

Sarah had surpassed the tithe suggested by her mother. She had entered the joyful space people inhabit when they follow Jesus' advice to care for the sick and the poor. She was not just giving money; she was investing in the work of the hospital, the way our family friend had invested start-up funds in her. Sarah saw herself as a steward of the wealth that her interests and talent had created. She found joy in giving. Her giving was significant, not only because of the amount of money she gave but as a way of blessing women and children in life-and-death circumstances. At that moment, Sarah defied gravity.

TITHING

In order to become stewards of financial resources, we have to accept the challenge of setting aside an amount of money to invest in the work of God's kingdom. Many Christians choose a practice from the Bible called tithing as a way to get serious about their desire to participate in what God is doing in the world. A tithe is one-tenth of one's income. As the children of Israel prepared to enter the Promised Land, they were instructed,

> When you cross over the Jordan and live in the land that the
> LORD your God is allotting to you, and when he gives you
> rest from your enemies all around so that you live in safety,
> then you shall bring everything that I command you to the
> place that the LORD your God will choose as a dwelling for
> his name: your burnt offerings and your sacrifices, your
> tithes and your donations, and all your choice votive gifts
> that you vow to the LORD. (Deuteronomy 12:10-11 NRSV)

Why would God ask the Israelites to do such a thing? It's not
as if the Almighty is short of funds or has lost the power to create
resources. Clearly, God is not in need of the tithe. It is possible that
the tithe is requested not for God's sake but for ours.

During the exodus, God provided a bread-like substance called
manna to sustain the people of Israel in the wilderness. They could
only collect enough manna for the day. Any excess would spoil and
rot. Over time they learned that they could trust God.

Now, as the people crossed into the Promised Land, they were
being called to trust God in a new way. God asked them to give
an amount of their income, the tithe, that could bless their community in a significant way, along with other offerings beyond the
tithe that would be given as well. The instruction was to give the
best of what they had first, before their wealth was used in other
ways. For example, they were not to give a sick lamb or a spoiled
batch of wine. From the beginning, generosity included sacrifice.
These acts of generosity taught the Israelites to honor God in the
present and to trust God for the future.

The tithe was used to support the worship life of Israel, but it
also had another purpose. It was used to take care of the most vulnerable people in the society:

> Every third year you shall bring out the full tithe of your produce for that year, and store it within your towns; the Levites, because they have no allotment or inheritance with you, as well as the resident aliens, the orphans, and the widows in your towns, may come and eat their fill so that the LORD your God may bless you in all the work that you undertake. (Deuteronomy 14:28-29 NRSV)

When I read of the ways the tithe supported the work of the Temple and the care of widows, orphans, and those from other countries who lived in Israel, it is clear that the tithe was intended to be a discipline that would enable people to take on their role in expanding God's kingdom. As people gave their tithe, they became God's servants. Through their generosity, they gained a sense of identity.

Most Christians who tithe today aren't doing so to follow the Law found in Leviticus; rather, this practice of proportional giving calls them to offer their best for the kingdom of God as a way to live into their identity as stewards.

Years ago I sat in the kitchen of a church member we all affectionately called Ms. Margaret who was in her early nineties. When the topic of giving came up, Ms. Margaret said how important giving was to her life and how much joy she found in tithing.

I glanced around her home. Ms. Margaret lived a simple life. She had a small house with a vegetable garden out back. She could usually be found in a wooden chair on the front porch. She would wave at neighbors who drove past. Looking around her kitchen, I could tell that everything there, from the pot on the stove to the clock on the wall, had been in service for many years.

I wondered how she had managed to tithe all those years. I worked up the courage to ask, "Ms. Margaret, it must have been difficult for you to have tithed. I know that you were never a wealthy person. And didn't your husband die before your children were grown?"

She smiled. Yes, it had been hard. The country was still recovering from the Great Depression. It was tough for a woman to find a job. She had to work and take care of the children. She kept a garden and was frugal in her spending, but she always wanted her children to see that giving was a part of their life. She said that she gave the tithe first and then lived on what was left.

One day Ms. Margaret was at a meeting of the Ladies Auxiliary at church, and an announcement was made that the annual missions offering would be collected in November. She came home sad, knowing she couldn't afford to contribute. There just wasn't a penny left over. Her son, noticing that his mother was sad, asked what was wrong. Ms. Margaret said she wanted to be part of the missions offering, but they wouldn't be able to contribute. Her son answered that if she wanted to give to that offering, they would do it together.

They put a mason jar on the kitchen table, and Ms. Margaret's son and daughter took odd jobs. They pulled weeds for the neighbors, then brought their pennies and nickels home and put them in the jar. Ms. Margaret took in sewing and put portions of the money in the jar. Bit by bit, nickels turned to dimes, and dimes to quarters. By the time November came around, they had a few dollars. Ms. Margaret took the children with her to the meeting, and together they put their offering on the table with everyone else's.

Ms. Margaret told me, "I think it was one of the proudest and happiest things we did together. That is why I like giving. It helped me teach my son and daughter who we were as a family. It helped them think about others. It was a blessing to us."

Listening to Ms. Margaret, I could sense the trust she had in God to provide for her needs. She didn't have many wants in this world. What she did have was a deep joy in giving.

Today, in the area where I live, children complain about what they don't have. Adults with good incomes and limited hardships struggle to find meaning and significance. And yet, the average person in America is better off than most people have been in the history of the earth. Access to clean water, sanitation, and indoor plumbing makes our standard of living higher than many of the greatest rulers of past civilizations. Some of us have more gadgets than we can count and willingly pay fees to sustain them at a level that previous generations would find astounding. We have access to more information on a smartphone than the world's greatest libraries contained only a few decades ago. Despite all that we possess, many of us lack the basic joy that Ms. Margaret and her children found when they placed a mason jar on the table and made generosity a part of their identity.

HARD TRUTHS

In *The Paradox of Generosity*, Christian Smith and Hilary Davidson

> review the data and find that very large numbers of Americans, despite wanting to enjoy joyful, healthy,

purposeful lives, fail to practice the kinds of generosity
that actually tend to lead to joy, health, and purpose in life.
Something gets in their way.[4]

The Science of Generosity survey, conducted by Smith in
2010, found that 44.8 percent of Americans reported giving $0
of their income to any charitable purpose. You read that right:
zero. Not one dollar. Nearly half of us gave away zip, nada, squat,
zilch. Nothing at all. These people apparently turned down Girl
Scouts, refused high school band collections, did a speed pass of
the offering plate at church, ignored the cancer research drive, told
the Salvation Army they had no change at Christmas, and then
said, "I didn't give at the office either!" This is not my judgment
(except that last part); it was self-reported. Another 41.3 percent
gave less than 2 percent of their income away. This means that the
vast majority of financial generosity in the United States is offered
by about 15 percent of the population, who are willing to give away
more than 2 percent of their income.[5]

You may be thinking, *At least people gave their time.* It's true that
volunteerism is extremely important to charitable organizations.
But in the same study, over 76 percent of the people self-
reported giving no volunteer hours to any organization. That is
three out of four people, a remarkable number. It seems that we are
experiencing a generosity famine.

The authors of the study observe,

> When it comes to generosity with money, time, skills, and
> relationships, we know that relaxing, letting go, and giving
> away is not often automatic or easy. This is especially true in
> American culture, which from all sides constantly pounds

home messages of scarcity, discontent, insecurity, and acquisition.[6]

It would be reasonable to assume that with the Bible's clear call to generosity and the example of those in the early church, the Christian community would offer a brighter picture. However, this assumption seems to be disproven in another book by Christian Smith, *Passing the Plate: Why American Christians Don't Give Away More Money* (with Michael O. Emerson and Patricia Snell). Smith and his coauthors present some hard truths about Christians in the United States that are corroborated by multiple data sources. One in five American Christians make no financial contribution to any charity at all, whether for religious or educational purposes or to relieve human suffering.[7]

The news does not get significantly better from there. The authors report that "according to the 1998 General Social Survey data, the amount of pre-tax household income contributed by the mean average American Christian is 2.9 percent." The survey showed that 72 percent of all Christians contribute less than 2 percent of their income to all causes, religious and not religious. Giving does improve with higher rates of church attendance, but even then the results demonstrate significantly lower amounts than we might expect. A full 45 percent of those who attend church two times a month or more give away less than 2 percent of their income. Only 9.4 percent of American Christians report giving 10 percent or more of their incomes to charitable causes."[8]

In *The Paradox of Generosity*, Smith and Davidson suggest that, like children whose fingers are caught in a Chinese finger trap, we pull frantically to find greater significance in life, but that simply keeps us stuck. It is only by relaxing and freely letting go of some resources that we can escape the trap.[9]

We are holding tight rather than letting go. Many of us who love God, want to honor Christ, and seek the will of the Holy Spirit in our lives have failed to move from receiving God's grace to participating in God's kingdom. In most cases, the issue is not that we lack desire; often those who don't give simply can't give. The issue is learning how to align our lives for generosity, and that's what we will talk about next.

3

TETHERED TO GOD

Honor the LORD with your wealth,
with the first of all your crops.
                                        (Proverbs 3:9)

3

TETHERED TO GOD

One of the greatest gravity-defying moments in history occurred on May 20, 1927, when Charles Lindbergh became the first person to fly an airplane from New York to Paris, France.

Lindbergh was just one of many in pursuit of the Orteig Prize, a $25,000 reward offered by hotel operator Raymond Orteig. It was a tremendous sum of money at the time. (Adjusted for inflation, it would be worth over $330,000 today.) Orteig wanted to advance aviation, and he knew that one way to do it would be to create a cash incentive to fly nonstop from New York to Paris, a goal that in 1927 seemed about as audacious as landing on the moon in the 1960s.

Several months earlier, French World War I flying ace René Fonck had risen to the challenge. Fonck's plane was as expansive as his personality. The interior was more like the living room of a chateau, with panels made of brushed aluminum, leather, and mahogany. There were chairs and a sofa that could be converted into a bed. He brought cases of wine and champagne, apparently forgetting that these were available in Paris. Before takeoff, he famously had a local hotel deliver a hot dinner that included clam chowder, terrapin, Long Island duck, and Vermont turkey. His plane, designed to carry no more than twenty thousand pounds, weighed in at whopping twenty-eight thousand pounds. He actually had to retrofit an extra wheel on the tail section to support the load. Think of packing your car for a vacation, then telling your family, *It'll be just a few more minutes—I have to add an extra wheel to support our gear!*

Thousands of spectators lined the airfield. Fonck pushed his plane as hard as he could, but even with an extended airstrip he never reached the critical speed for takeoff. The plane hit a bump when it crossed a service road. As the *New York Times* reported, "The plane began to shed parts as if it was a rickety old automobile coming to pieces."[1] At the end of the runway Fonck's doomed plane made its way over a small incline, toppled forward and burst into flames. Fonck and his navigator made it out, but the other two members of his crew did not.[2]

Another team that may have had the best chance of claiming the Orteig Prize included airplane manufacturer Giuseppe Bellanca and millionaire Charles Levine. Bellanca produced a prototype called *Columbia*. Levine wanted the flight of the *Columbia* to be a spectacle and would spare no expense or conflict to do so. Rather than having a navigator to chart the course, Levine decided to hire two pilots then planned to choose one on the runway the day of the flight by drawing lots. His goal was to attract greater publicity. Later, Levine wanted to fire one of the pilots, because he didn't think the man was handsome enough for newsreels and photos.

Eventually Levine chose Clarence Chamberlin and Lloyd Bertraud as his crew. Levine, Bellanca, and the crew disagreed greatly on virtually everything from the flight plan to the equipment. Just when it seemed things could not get more dysfunctional, Levine presented Chamberlin and Bertraud with contracts the night before takeoff, stipulating that they would receive just a small salary, while Levine would receive the prize money and any funds from a post-flight tour. The two bewildered aviators reluctantly signed the contract. The next morning, Bertraud literally woke up to what he had done the night before and found an attorney to file a temporary injunction preventing the flight. The team was grounded as Lindbergh continued his preparations.[3]

Commander Richard E. Byrd was also in the running. Byrd was the American Naval officer who claimed to have reached the North Pole in 1926. He was funded by department store owner Rodman Wannamaker. Byrd and Wannamaker both valued safety and took their time to insure it. Byrd wanted to fly from New York to Paris, but he was very clear that he would not be rushed, prize or no prize. He took every safety device you could find in 1927 and sometimes carried two for the sake of redundancy, including rations, water, extra clothes, a radio, and two rubber rafts. He even had a two-piece bamboo pole with a red flag on top to use on the rafts.

On one of Byrd's many trials, his plane was damaged on landing and had to be substantially repaired. It seems as though the failed landing only reinforced Wanamaker's insistence that Byrd run more and more tests on his plane. As a result, when Lindbergh took off for Paris, Byrd still had not attempted his own trip and even shook Lindbergh's hand as Lindbergh boarded his plane. Byrd remained behind doing inspections and test flights for nine more days before he departed for Paris.[4]

As for Charles Lindbergh, what he lacked in personnel, security, and supplies he more than made up for in focus. Lindbergh had no navigator, copilot, or crew to go along on his trip. He worked with a team of financial backers whose main contribution, he later said, was to provide the funding and leave the rest to him. He wanted to be the first person to fly from New York to Paris and claim the prize, and he was personally involved in every aspect of the trip. He worked closely with Ryan aircraft to give input about the design of the plane, which they named *The Spirit of St. Louis*. Wanting a plane that was as stable and light as possible, he said, "A plane that's got to break the world's record for nonstop flying should be stripped of every excess ounce of weight."[5]

As a result, his plane had only one engine, to conserve fuel. It had one seat for one pilot, to save weight. There were no luxuries, not even a forward windshield, so Lindbergh had to navigate using the side window and a periscope. He carried a small raft but left behind his radio and parachute.[6]

Lindbergh lifted off from Roosevelt Field in New York, and 33½ hours later he landed at Le Bourget Field near Paris, 3,600 miles away. He was greeted by thousands of cheering people. The press dubbed him Lucky Lindy, but his success was by no means an accident. It was the result of singular focus, by which Lindbergh marshaled his resources, oversaw construction of his plane, set his course carefully, and then executed his plan flawlessly, serving as both pilot and navigator.[7]

PLANNING FOR GENEROSITY

Charles Lindbergh's pursuit of the Orteig Prize was gravity defying, but how does it relate to a book on generosity? Effective generosity, like Lindbergh's flight, does not just happen. It's the result of thoughtful planning and design. Though 46 percent of US citizens gave no money to charitable organizations of any kind, we can be certain that many wish they had given and hope to be generous in the future. But that requires goals to be set and plans to be executed. Being generous in an effective way means being dedicated to giving, the way Lindbergh and his colleagues were dedicated to aviation. When you read the stories of these men, it's clear that being a pilot was not an interest or vocation; it was an identity.

The problem is not that people are miserly or mean. Quite the opposite. Most people want to be openhanded and actively compassionate. They want to respond to real opportunities for doing good and using their time and money to make the world a better place. The problem is that we are like the competitors for the Orteig Prize.

Some of us, like Fonck, are so weighed down by the gravity of possessions that we are not able to experience the freedom of generosity. Worse than that, our financial wheels are often coming off as we motor down the runway of life. Others of us, like Byrd, are so concerned about personal security that we avoid or bypass the great goals of generosity. We inspect and reinspect our assets and liabilities, and so we remain grounded. Still others of us are like Levine. All the assets are in place, but with competing financial goals, conflicting personal values, and poor communication skills, especially on the topic of money, we struggle to break free from the culture of more. As a result, we never experience the exhilaration of the journey.

Generous people understand that blessing others with time, talent, and money requires the same kind of focus and intentionality that Charles Lindbergh demonstrated in accomplishing his historic flight. Generosity does not happen by accident. To make a real contribution with time or money, we need to think about what we hope to accomplish, plan a strategy that fits our time and finances, and then muster the courage to act.

I have talked to many financially generous people over the years, and nearly all of them say it's important to do three things: make a budget, live simply, and set goals for generosity.

MAKE A BUDGET

Making a budget reminds us that our entire financial world is relevant to our faith in God. If God is truly central to our lives, we must begin a budget by planning what we will invest in the work of God's kingdom. If we do not plan this first, we will simply be offering God the leftovers. And by the time our other bills have been paid, often the leftovers are nonexistent. Discipleship cannot begin with the contribution we make after other bills are paid.

When God is central to our lives, we begin to analyze *all* our expenses and financial plans in light of God's desires for us. We create a false dichotomy when we divide our financial world between what we spend on ourselves and what we offer to God. This can create a sense of guilt over personal expenditures, from rent or mortgage expenses for our home to car expenses for needed transportation.

But the guilt is unwarranted. The Bible is clear that we are to provide for our needs and those of our family. Seen this way, supplying food, shelter, clothing, and other basics of life for ourselves and others is itself an act of generosity. Such provision creates a safe environment, where we can generously use our gifts and graces for others because our own needs are being met. It creates a place of safety and even abundance where marriages can prosper and children can grow and thrive. Paul states in clear terms that people need to care for the members of their family, especially if those members are vulnerable, as widows in his time also would have been. So, budgeting for needs such as food and housing is a facet of being generous. Paul tells Timothy,

> Teach these things so that the families will be without fault. But if someone doesn't provide for their own family, and especially for a member of their household, they have denied the faith. They are worse than those who have no faith. (1 Timothy 5:7-8)

Paul calls on church members to create homes that are a blessing to those who dwell in them. Budget expense categories enable us to think through the reasonable allocation of our income to each facet of our life. Essential areas of a family or personal budget correspond to passages in the Bible that envision a preferred future for God's people.

The prophet Isaiah, for example, painted a stark picture of coming hardship for the people of Israel. He spoke of a deserted king's palace, an abandoned city, and fields and vineyards that produced only briars. Then he painted a contrasting picture of the same land where the Spirit of God is present, when "a spirit from on high is poured out on us.... Then my people will live in a peaceful dwelling, in secure homes, in carefree resting places" (Isaiah 32:15a, 18). Such places, where there is relational harmony and everyone has enough, are all part of God's intention for us.

We live God's way when we provide for our needs and create enough financial margin to bring us a more carefree life. Budgets help make that vision a reality, and they give us the ability to contribute to the needs of others or to organizations that seek greater justice in the world. If you currently provide for yourself or your family and are not going into debt each month to do so, you are already well on your way to a fully generous life.

The Bible can be helpful regarding budget categories and how to balance them. The psalmist alludes to the balance of life that allows a godly person to both provide for their household and be generous:

> I was young and now I'm old,
> > but I have never seen the righteous left all alone,
> > have never seen their children begging for bread.
> They are always gracious and generous.
> > Their children are a blessing. (Psalm 37:25-26)

Clothing, another budget category, is found at the very beginning of the Bible, when God prepares Adam and Eve for their departure from Eden. "The LORD God made the man and his wife leather clothes and dressed them" (Genesis 3:21).

References to savings are found in the wisdom literature and point us to logic found in the natural world.

> Go to the ant, you lazy person;
>> observe its ways and grow wise.
> The ant has no commander, officer, or ruler.
>> Even so, it gets its food in summer;
>> gathers its provisions at harvest. (Proverbs 6:6-8)

Expenses related to education are also consistent with the Bible's guidance, since knowledge is seen as a necessary part of sustaining a good life. "Wisdom's protection is like the protection of money; the advantage of knowledge is that wisdom preserves the lives of its possessors" (Ecclesiastes 7:12).

Passages such as these show us the importance of budgeting to provide for our lives and the lives of family members, while enabling us to work for compassion and justice in our community and world.

This is not a book on how to budget, but there are many excellent resources available to assist you in that task. The key observation here is that when we meet the basic needs of life, our money is being used in ways that are consistent with the wisdom and practices described in the Bible. We are in concert with God's will. Meeting those needs will allow us to look at a level of spending that is pleasing to God in each budget category so we can balance our resources accordingly.

Our generosity to others will not happen by accident. It can happen, however, when we become serious about being stewards of our income and make appropriate allocations in every area of our finances. We gain that ability when we create and live within the boundaries of a budget.

LIVE SIMPLY

Remember Lindbergh's willingness to fly light and stay focused on the goal? In similar fashion, people who successfully live within the guidelines of their budget often maintain a rule that centers their life: *Keep it simple.* I have observed this quality at work in the buying decisions of many generous people I have known over the years. It cuts across all income brackets. Although wealthy individuals have a great deal more income and assets, they often keep life simple in terms of actual possessions.

This was discovered years ago by Thomas Stanley and William Danko, authors of *The Millionaire Next Door.* They found that people of high net worth often live in average homes, drive used cars, and don't wear the most expensive clothes. They have a clear vision of the difference between *needs* and *wants.* Most of these people gained their wealth through careful attention to how much money moves in and out of their businesses. They do the same at home. The disciplines of frugality, saving, and using a budget often push them toward the practice of simplicity. I believe that simplicity is the most effective tool people can employ if they want to escape the financial gravity of our culture.[8]

Gravity-bound people usually see simplicity as the absence of life's good things, such as a new car, a bigger home, or the latest consumer goods. In this view, simplicity makes no sense; it represents a commitment to all our worst assumptions about a monastic lifestyle. The bed is hard. The car is undependable. The shirt is haircloth. Dinner is a meager fare of hard bread and cold vegetables. The house is small and in bad repair. Because people see simplicity as absence, there is no motivation to practice it. The good stuff, they assume, is inside the ads on the computer screen or the deals offered by local retailers. Gravity-bound people pursue these things with abandon, believing they offer a path to the good life.

This is why many of us inexplicably find our cabinets, drawers, closets, basements, attics, and sometimes rented off-site units full of stuff and more stuff. All that consumption leaves a trail.

Believe it or not, the same problem exists in outer space. Every year, countries around the globe send up rockets and payloads on missions to outer space. Each of these space missions leaves things behind that go into orbit around Earth. When one piece of space junk collides with another, it produces new debris. When you consider the vast size of the area around Earth, this would not seem like a problem. But the more crowded it gets, the more complicated life becomes for those using the "space" of space. Right now, there are over twenty thousand pieces of old spacecraft, used rocket parts, and dead satellites orbiting the earth. Like the junk that occupies that back room of your basement, these things have not been used in years. When you include smaller fragments—anything larger than a marble—the number of pieces goes up to over 500,000. To make matters worse, they travel at speeds up to 17,500 miles an hour. At that velocity, even tiny bits of paint from these debris have damaged windows on the space shuttle.[9]

Which brings us back to our world. Not only do our stored possessions take up space but they often give us a sense of regret as we wonder what mission we were on when these items came into our lives. The electronic ab exerciser, that box of Happy Meal toys, the paperweight collection, a tarnished candlestick, games that look new because no one played them, molded plastic sleds that promised fun but didn't slide, seldom-played musical instruments—all these things seemed like good ideas at the time. Now they are space junk. Not used for years, these items still possess their old gravity, so it can be hard for people to recycle them or donate them to a thrift store. This is a life of complexity, not simplicity, in which we must constantly adjust to keep from bumping into all of that stuff. Did ownership of these items really equate the good life?

Consumption has consequences. Experts estimate that about one in six Americans suffers from an anxiety disorder for a variety of reasons, one of which appears to be related to our possessions. To reduce anxiety, items are purchased. That releases hormones in our brain that make us feel pleasure. When the items are brought home, however, the clutter level rises. This brings more anxiety, which starts the cycle over again. This is gravity at its worst, pulling us into its vortex. The effect can feel both inescapable and crushing.[10]

A whole industry has grown up around the American practice of being consumed by consumption. Stores have popped up that sell nothing but containers for our stuff. We can hire a professional organizer who will make us put our things in stacks in the driveway. The stack of things to be thrown out can be picked up by another business that will complete the cycle by hauling it to the landfill. In the past decade, one of the country's fastest growing companies has been 1-800-GOT-JUNK.

At the church I serve we offered a Saturday when people could recycle and give away their space junk. Nonprofits brought big trucks to pick up stuff to be resold. An electronic recycler took old computers. A giant shredder safely destroyed documents. Watching people unload their cars, vans, and trucks, I began to notice something about the people. They were all so happy. They had big smiles on their faces. They profusely thanked the volunteers who set up the event. Several people talked about how great it was to clean out the house. It occurred to me that they may have had more joy getting rid of the stuff than they had when they first purchased it.

Here's why: gravity-defiers see simplicity as freedom—from the pressures of debt and clutter, and from the complexity of having more than one needs. When these people talk about living a simple life, they say it's less about rules and guidelines and more about discovering what brings us fulfillment. It's true of time or money. When choosing how to spend time, we often get busier and busier as we take on more responsibilities, hoping to find a sense of significance. To gain simplicity, we need to identify things that bring us real joy in life and allow these to weed out everything else. In other words, it's not about denying ourselves things that might bring us happiness; it's about avoiding things that keep us from the deepest joy.

We hope that more money and possessions will make life better. But the more we have to maintain and the more expensive those items are, the more financial stress we will experience. The key is to find what brings us joy and then order our life around it. Simplicity allows us to drop tangential pursuits and expenses, freeing us up to pursue what matters to us. In the process, thoughts of what we once longed to possess will be crowded out, helping us overcome sins related to financial gravity, such as greed or covetousness.

In the days of old, before the invention of the GPS and other navigational systems, sailors set their course by the stars. They looked in the sky and saw star after star after star. But here is what they discovered: You can't navigate using a multiplicity of constellations; you have to find the North Star and set your course by it. That one star will guide your journey to the destination you seek. For Christians, Jesus is true north. His vision of God's kingdom as an experience of love, compassion, and justice is the one thing we are called to pursue. Jesus put it this way:

> "No one can serve two masters. Either you will hate the one and love the other, or you will be loyal to the one and have contempt for the other. You cannot serve God and wealth."
>
> (Matthew 6:24-25)

The principle of simplicity, which leads people to see the difference between needs and wants, enables us to avoid serving wealth. Simplicity helps us to be content with what we have. No longer do we feel a need to have newer and better. Suddenly electronic devices have a longer life. Cars last long after the final payment is made. Houses may be improved over the years, but they don't have to be greatly expanded or sold for a bigger place across town. Children are taught to be happy with fewer toys and to show greater appreciation for birthday or holiday gifts.

If we have Jesus as our true north, we will live generous lives no matter where we go. If friends call and ask to talk, we will make time. If we hear of a way to bless others in the community, we will offer help. If we see people who are hungry, we will buy them food.

If we don't have Christ as our true north, every shiny star will redirect our course for new waters. Every visit to the Internet or walk through the mall will beckon us to a spending harbor. It is so easy to be pulled off course. Maybe that's what Paul meant when he wrote to Timothy, "Tell people who are rich at this time not to become egotistical and not to place their hope on their finances, which are uncertain. Instead, they need to hope in God, who richly provides everything for our enjoyment" (1 Timothy 6:17).

You may be thinking, *That doesn't apply to me, because I'm not rich.* But if Timothy brought his first-century congregation to your house right now, imagine what they would say.

"You have indoor plumbing? Seriously? Your house is cool in the summer and warm in the winter? You have running water and can drink it from the faucet? There's a bus that takes you to work every day? There's a device that helps you speak to people across town or around the world? That's amazing! The Emperor of Rome doesn't have such things!"

When we put our hope in God and make Jesus our North Star, we count our blessings and see how God has provided for us in so many ways. Soon the allure of more and better loses its appeal, and we begin to seek other goals.

Living simply enables us to focus on Paul's advice to Timothy: "Tell them to do good, to be rich in the good things they do, to be generous, and to share with others" (1 Timothy 6:18).

SET GOALS FOR GENEROSITY

Besides making a budget and living simply, financially generous people suggest setting numerical goals for the good they hope to do with their time and money. They pray about God's calling in their lives. They consider which of their activities bring joy to God and also bring joy uniquely to them. Then they find ways to participate. As these activities are discerned, financial goals are projected for their annual giving, along with metrics by which to measure them.

When we are generous, we aren't so much doing things for God as we are becoming part of what God is doing in the world. As stewards, we understand that resources ultimately belong to the Lord, and we simply manage them. That's why it's important to begin the year with quantifiable goals of what we hope to contribute to the ministries, organizations, and projects to which God calls us. It's amazing what we can do when we set goals for financial generosity and then order our lives to make that generosity possible.

Ask pastors which members financially enable the ministry of their church, and they will tell you about people living on average and fixed incomes who tithe. Most churches are not supported by one or two wealthy benefactors but by a cadre of committed members who find joy in a vital ministry. They want to see the church share the Christian faith with a new generation in Sunday school or student ministry. They are pleased to hear that their church has helped a homeless person find housing or welcomed a new member into the life of the congregation. They get excited when more church members study the Bible or when a new sound system enables people to hear the sermon or communion liturgy more clearly. The church uses their money to do everything from supporting mission work abroad to repainting the sign out front. For people who give, these things bring joy, and that joy is the reason they arrange their budget so they can live a full life and still give generously.

Through their church or beyond it, they will find ways to bless those around them. Often the reason for this generosity is connected to the story of their life. A person who went to college on scholarship gives funds to support deserving students. A woman who grew up in a foster home donates to a program assisting vulnerable children. A man who is deeply concerned about the environment gives time and money to clean up a local river. Generosity becomes an experience of gain rather than loss when we find the place where our joy overlaps God's will.

Inevitably someone will say, "I can't do that. I can't afford it." Consider Albert Lexie, a shoeshine man. Lexie has shined shoes since 1957 and has worked inside Pittsburgh's Children Hospital for over thirty years. He charges five dollars for a shoeshine and then donates all his tips to a fund that assists sick children whose parents can't afford to pay medical costs. Lexie says that most of his tips are between one and two dollars. You may wonder whether the tips of a shoeshine man, no matter how well-intentioned, could make much difference. According to the hospital administration, Lexie brings in a few hundred dollars every week. Over a thirty-year period he has given over $200,000 to help sick kids. He is a major benefactor to the hospital. That level of generosity only comes when you discern the nature of God's calling over your life.[11]

Lexie was one of thirteen people honored by the Caring Institute in 2006. The Caring Awards, inspired by the work of Mother Teresa of Calcutta, recognize people who have shown commitment to charitable activities and have set an example for others. Beneficiaries that year included Dr. Ben Carson, Rev. Billy Graham, and baseball great Cal Ripken, Jr. Think about those people: a noted neurologist who became a presidential candidate, perhaps the greatest evangelist since the Apostle Paul, the Iron Man of baseball, and a shoeshine man from Pittsburgh. Albert Lexie's name on that list is proof that when we set goals for generosity, all of us can make a difference. It's not about your title or fame; it's about your diligence and desire to bless the lives of others in a real way.[12]

Paul talks about the result of generosity when he states, "When they do these things, they will save a treasure for themselves that is a good foundation for the future. That way they can take hold of what is truly life" (1 Timothy 6:19).

Paul's biggest worry is that if you and I are not careful, we will settle for a life that's held down by the gravity of our culture and miss the abundant life promised to us in Christ. In our heart of hearts, we don't want an ordinary life; we long for the extraordinary, the transcendent.

Recently I spoke to a guy who was going skydiving. He told me, "If it doesn't go well, look for me on CNN." I said, "I hate to tell you this, but if it doesn't go well you probably won't make it onto CNN—more like the local news at 5:00."

All kidding aside, why was he taking the risk of skydiving? He was pursuing life. He didn't want a normal, boring existence. He wanted to tell stories about excitement and joy, and he was happy to jump out of an airplane to do so.

Many of us are living a life that feels not only boring but somehow enclosed, even imprisoned. As you read this, hear Paul when he says, "Tell them to do good, to be rich in the good things they do, to be generous, and to share with others. When they do these things, they will save a treasure for themselves that is a good foundation for the future" (1 Tim 6:18-19).

God wants you to have a life that is truly life. Generosity is the path. If you have it as a goal, you can defy gravity and cross the great distance from committed consumer to generous steward.

4

WHEN WE GET IT RIGHT

*Do not store up for yourselves treasures on
earth, where moths and vermin destroy,
and where thieves break in and steal.
But store up for yourselves treasures in
heaven, where moths and vermin do not
destroy, and where thieves do not break
in and steal. For where your treasure is,
there your heart will be also.*

(Matthew 6:19-21 NIV)

4

WHEN WE GET IT RIGHT

My interest in writing a book about generosity and Christian stewardship is based on the powerful way this discipline has shaped my life in Christ. I experienced the impact of financial gravity the way most people do: early and often. My two older brothers and I grew up with parents who took us to church unless we were running a temperature over 100 degrees. It's hard to fake a fever, which I discovered when I put the thermometer on a hot light bulb.

"Well," my mom said, "I'll need to take you to the hospital. The doctor has probably never seen anyone alive with 110-degree temperature, so this should be of some interest."

When our parents provided us with money to put in the offering plate at church, giving was easy. It was bit more challenging when they started us on a small allowance and said it was important to give a portion to the church. I would carefully decide how many pennies to take to church. Sometimes I even dropped a full nickel into the offering plate! I beamed with pride as I shared my largesse for the greater good.

When I was eleven years old, I began delivering papers six afternoons a week. It was not an easy job. The papers had to be rolled and placed in either the wire baskets on my bike or a large canvas sack that I carried around my neck. I was a thin boy, no more than eighty pounds—all arms and legs with little coordination to connect them. When my bike was fully loaded with 135 newspapers, it felt like I was trying to drive a Harley-Davidson Road King with side bags. Find a photo of a Harley-Davidson, draw a stick figure on it, and you'll get the idea. A quick turn or ill-considered stop would lead to a bad encounter with gravity.

Delivering *The Winchester Evening Star* required the fidelity of an Alaskan sled dog in the winter and the diligence of a Grand Canyon pack mule in the summer. The work included hazards. Rain meant each paper had to be wrapped in plastic, and your bike tires were more likely to slip on the wet streets. Snow meant the route would have to be completed on foot. The growling mastiff on Ridge Avenue, so tall that he stared at me eyeball to eyeball as he charged and barked, was only slightly more intimidating than the excited St. Bernard on Caroline Street, whose joyful greeting would easily unseat me.

My monthly income as a paper carrier was just over thirty-five dollars. I still recall the satisfaction I felt at the arrival of my paycheck and the careful planning that went into spending that money. I was flush with cash. Candy bar? No problem. New poster for my room? Go for it. Save for a camera? Easily done. It was exciting to think of the options my income presented. That paper route helped me connect the dots of work, income, and buying power. It changed my self-image. Suddenly I was a man of business. I had the power to buy things without asking my parents or saving my paltry allowance for months.

One day my mom and dad asked me what I was going to do with my money. I told them about things I wanted to buy, and we discussed how best to save for larger items so I wouldn't squander my resources on smaller ones. Then they asked, "What do you plan to give to God?"

The word *give* triggered something in my mind. *Give,* as in *give away,* as in *not have it anymore,* as in *have nothing to show for it.* When I thought of buying things, I imagined a collection of treasures that my hard work had earned. But when I heard the word *give,* all I could think of was loss.

"Just give it away?" I asked.

My parents explained that every week they gave away a percentage of their income to God through the church, and they found it to be a real source of joy. I knew they put something in the offering plate each week, but until that moment it didn't occur to me that they just gave away their money. I could not have been more dumbfounded if they had suddenly started speaking a foreign language.

83

Then they upped the ante. "You know," said my dad, "now that you're working you have the ability to make a real offering each week. A lot of Christians use 10 percent as a guide for what they give to God. That would be about $3.50 a month for you."

Give $3.50 a month? I pictured this vast sum suddenly being wiped away. It was one thing to squander a month's work on candy bars, soft drinks, movie tickets, and whoopee cushions; it was quite another simply to give it away for who knows what. Buying felt like gain. Saving felt good because it would allow me to buy bigger things later. But giving? That was a different matter altogether. It might be what good people and good Christians did, but—make no mistake about it—giving felt like losing.

LEARNING TO BE GENEROUS

That was the first time I felt the pull of financial gravity. It's been many years since I had that paper route, and what I've discovered is that money management is only one place where I struggle with generosity. There are times when I have trouble being generous with other character traits—patience with a child, time with a person in need, volunteer hours during a busy week. Sometimes I struggle to show compassion when I see the needs of my community and the world, to listen as someone shares a hardship they're facing, to extend forgiveness to others. I can think of times when I've been stingy with love, grace, and a host of other qualities that would be normative for a person who follows Jesus Christ.

That's why learning to be generous is such an important part of the Christian life. Generosity is a means of grace in the process

84

of Christian sanctification. We simply will never grow in the love of Christ unless we allow God to form a generous spirit within us.

Financial generosity is a helpful starting point, because it exposes in many of us a resistance to giving. There are many spiritual disciplines that the Holy Spirit uses to form and sanctify our character. Worship, prayer, study, and service would all be good examples. But I've found that giving weekly, starting with a tithe, is one of the most significant practices in my life, one I'm now grateful I was dragged into, kicking and screaming, as a boy.

When I asked my wife, Karen, to marry me, she joyfully agreed, but I soon learned the full meaning of partnership. Karen tithed when she was single and planned to continue offering a minimum of 10 percent of our earnings to God each year in our married life.

Karen had become a Christian in college through a campus ministry, and her faith had been nurtured by a church that did a great job teaching basic practices of the Christian life. She was a disciplined person, so when they taught her to pray, she prayed. When they taught her to read the Bible and join a small group for study and discussion, she read and attended faithfully. When they told her that service to others would help her meet Jesus, she served joyfully. When they encouraged her to worship weekly, she showed up willingly. So when they taught her to tithe, she enjoyed the opportunity to give to God. It was not easy. She worked two or three jobs to pay tuition and living expenses while she attended classes, and she could have put off tithing until she was out of school or had her first full-time job. But she didn't wait. She gave the church 10 percent of her small income without reservation.

Karen knew what life was like without Christ, and she knew what life was like with Christ. A tithe felt like a small amount to give if it would help the church lead others to the life of discipleship she enjoyed. More than that, she liked what giving did in her personal life. It was a tangible way to remember, week after week, that she was dependent on God for all that she had. It reminded her that God sustained her and that God was trustworthy. Karen understood what the writer of the Psalm expressed:

> So I called on the LORD's name:
> "LORD, please save me!"
>
> The LORD is merciful and righteous;
> our God is compassionate.
> The LORD protects simple folk;
> he saves me whenever I am brought down.
> I tell myself, You can be at peace again,
> because the LORD has been good to you.
>
> (Psalm 116:4-7)

Karen had been the recipient of God's generous love and grace as well as God's provision for her needs in life. As a result, she wanted to participate in what God was doing in the world. She wanted to become a person who was generous.

When Karen said the practice of tithing would need to be a part of our life together as a married couple, I joyfully accepted her terms. My quick response wasn't because of her faith or theology or the opportunity to serve God. It was because I was in love. She could have said I had to wake up every morning, paint myself green, and pretend to be a head of broccoli, and I still would have said yes. What guy who considers himself a Christian and is in love could resist the simple request of tithing?

Six months later, the weekend after our wedding, Karen and I sat together in a worship service in Decatur, Georgia. She had found a job as a teacher and was taking evening classes in graduate school while I attended seminary full-time. Money was tight, to say the least. During the worship service, Karen saw that the offering was about to be collected. She pulled *our* checkbook from her purse. I recall the joy I felt that morning. I had a college degree. I was in church with my wife. We had a checkbook. Our names were on the checks. We were about to give the first offering of our married life. I was officially an adult. I felt a surge of gratitude and thanksgiving.

Karen wrote the check, tore it out, and handed it to me to put into the plate. I was stunned by the figure on the check. I had never given that much money to an offering in my life. The ushers were approaching. I wasn't sure what to do. If I dropped the check into the plate, all that money would be gone. If I held it, I knew Karen would not be pleased. She saw the confusion on my face and motioned for me to place the check in the offering plate. I froze. I held the check above the plate but couldn't will my fingers to release it. The usher shook the plate a bit to prompt me. I looked at him with questioning eyes. He reached out and tried to take the check from my hands. As he tugged, I pulled back. He pulled harder until the check slipped from my fingertips.

Okay, that last part didn't happen, but it was exactly how it felt when I dropped the check into the plate. I was immediately resentful of the amount of money on the check, the offering, the offering plate, and the fact that the usher was proceeding nonchalantly up the aisle with our personal fortune. The offering converted my brief moment of thanksgiving into a day of sullenness.

I don't recall anything else about that service. I'm sure there was an anthem and a hymn and a sermon, but I didn't hear anything else that morning. When Karen and I walked out of church, the conversation went something like this:

I said, "What was that?!"

She said, "What are you talking about?"

"I'm talking about the amount of the check! What was that?"

She smiled. "Oh, that was our tithe! If you take my salary for the past two weeks and multiply by 10 percent, that's how much we put into the offering plate. Isn't it great?"

It didn't seem great. It seemed like a good way to go broke. The contrast between our experiences that morning was profound. Karen gave the offering with joy. She liked being generous and felt that our tithe was just a beginning. She was buoyant. I felt weighed down by the cash represented in that check, as though I had lost some of my dearest friends. I felt heavy and dense. When we parked the car and went up to our apartment, she bounced up the stairs. I plodded along behind her.

It took me about five years of marriage to my generous wife before I was able to enter her world, and when I finally did, the spiritual discipline she offered me changed my life. I realized that I had not matured much over the years. The reluctance to commit to generosity that was found in the preteen paperboy was still present in the college graduate.

I recall one of the times I suggested that we back off our tithe so our budget wouldn't be so tight. Karen stopped what she was doing, shook her head, and said, "Tom, you'll really have to figure out this giving thing if you plan to become a pastor. Pastors have to ask other people to give their money to the church, and I'm just not sure how you can do that when you find it so difficult yourself."

I had to concede that she had a point. But Karen knew that something much larger was at stake than a few authentic stewardship sermons. Since giving is an expression of our love for God, Karen knew that if I didn't change, I would never have the happiness and freedom we experience when we live in tandem with God. I would never mature into the person God wanted me to be until I took on the identity of God's steward.

At first I simply followed Karen's lead in generosity. Sometimes the best discipleship you have to offer is to follow the happy person and keep your grumbling to yourself. That period of time was a spiritual internship of sorts. I lived out the old adage that you can fake it till you make it. Here is what I learned:

- God can be trusted when financial surprises come into our lives. I was amazed when some small but adequate provision for our necessities would appear at the necessary moment.
- There is a difference between needs and wants.
- If you ask, God will take away your longing for more.
- Our offering is an investment in the work of God's kingdom.

One day I realized I wasn't following anymore. My understanding and experiences with giving were no longer lived vicariously through my wife; they were my own. Rather than working to catch up with Karen from behind, I could enjoy the view as I walked beside her. I had my own conviction and testimony to the freedom and joy found in being a steward of God's blessings. I found that I could defy gravity.

Besides finding personal satisfaction, I learned that the disciplines of saving and tithing had bound us together as a couple, freeing us from arguments over money, possessions, and finances. The practice of tithing helped me surrender more and more territory from the kingdom of self to the kingdom of God.

Generosity has played a profound role in my Christian transformation, enabling me to depend more fully upon God and celebrate what Christ is doing in the world. One of my greatest joys now is to join with others who also enjoy giving their time, talent, and finances so that together we can help advance God's kingdom here on earth. In many ways, the practice of generosity gave me purpose in life. In so doing, it freed me from many of the concerns and anxieties I had carried. It changed more than my checkbook; it changed my identity and character to that of a steward.

A STEWARD NAMED JOSEPH

Perhaps the greatest example of a steward in the Bible is Joseph. Joseph's life had a rough start that was no fault of his own. His father, Jacob, had two wives, Leah and Rachel, who were sisters. This marital arrangement, combined with a highly flawed ancient practice that valued women based primarily on the number of male children they bore, laid the foundation for one very messed-up family system.

Year after year, Rachel watched her sister Leah put points on the board by delivering babies. Everyone knew Jacob favored Rachel, but it wasn't much consolation to Rachel, who was saddened by her seeming inability to have children. Then one day it happened. Rachel became pregnant, carried the baby to term, and delivered a son whom they named Joseph. Joseph was a celebrated child and the apple of his father's eye. Just to make sure everyone knew, Jacob had an ornate coat made for Joseph, while his brothers walked around in hand-me-downs. Being the favored son seemed to stunt Joseph's social awareness. He told his brothers that he had odd dreams. In one, they were all stalks of grain. While his stalk stood tall, their stalks bowed down to him. In another dream his family members were the sun, moon, and stars. They all bowed down to him again.

For Joseph's brothers, the dreams were the final straw. They grabbed Joseph, threw him into a pit, and sold him to slave traders. They put blood on his fancy coat and told their father that animals had killed him. Jacob was heartbroken. One can imagine Joseph in a counselor's office years later recalling this scene after being asked, "When did you first suspect that your family was dysfunctional?..."

This story is well known to most who have read the Bible or seen the Broadway play about Joseph. Don't let familiarity blind you to how abysmally Joseph's brothers treated him. By all rights there should have been no recovery from that moment.

But God has amazing redemptive capacity. A man named Potiphar, a captain in the Egyptian army, purchased Joseph, and in Potiphar's home Joseph discovered his identity. Even though he had lost everything, Joseph became a steward of his master's home and possessions. "Potiphar thought highly of Joseph, and Joseph became his assistant; he appointed Joseph head of his household and put everything he had under Joseph's supervision" (Genesis 39:4).

Joseph was careful with Potiphar's resources, making sure the needs of the household were met. It is obvious that Joseph loved God, even during those dark years. He honored God by demonstrating his personal integrity. He was honest. He did not steal. He was diligent with Potiphar's assets and pleased to be of service. Joseph was tested when Potiphar's wife tried to seduce him. When he refused her offer, she told everyone he had made an unwanted advance and he was thrown into prison.

In prison, Joseph helped others by interpreting their dreams. In addition, he pursued his identity as a steward, demonstrating that he was trustworthy and able to manage others: "The jail's commander put all of the prisoners in the jail under Joseph's supervision, and he was the one who determined everything that happened there" (Genesis 39:22).

Joseph did not let his circumstances dictate his faith or character. He did not give up because his circumstances were unjust, nor did he refuse to assist the jail's commander because of his wrongful imprisonment. Joseph did not wait for better circumstances; he simply offered his best to the world and to God. He used the gifts God had provided and the character God was forging to manage the jail. He was dependable, honest, and effective. Joseph was a steward.

Joseph's ability to interpret dreams eventually brought him to the attention of the pharaoh of Egypt, who was having odd dreams. Joseph helped the pharaoh understand that God was telling him something: the pharoah would have seven years to prepare for a famine that would devastate Egypt and the surrounding regions. Because Joseph was a practiced steward, he was able to offer a strategy to prepare for the famine. Pharaoh was impressed. Then Pharaoh said to Joseph, "Since God has made all this known to you, no one is as intelligent and wise as you are. You will be in charge of my kingdom, and all my people will obey your command" (Genesis 41:39-40).

Years later, after Joseph built had great storehouses and filled them with grain and other food, the years of famine began. As forecast, the famine struck not only Egypt but the surrounding regions as well. Because of Joseph's efforts, Egypt was the only territory prepared for the famine, with storehouses of grain to see them through.

One day during the famine, Joseph's brothers showed up in Egypt, hoping to buy food for their starving families. Once again Joseph was decked out in a fancy coat. He also had the pharaoh's signet ring, a gold necklace, and a fine chariot. Joseph was doing so well that his brothers didn't recognize him. They bowed before him and asked if they could buy food.

It was a moment full of possibilities. Here were the men, his own brothers, who had sold him into slavery. Joseph had suffered years as a slave and prisoner. Everything had been taken from him. Now he was in charge. He could have taken revenge or retribution. He could have ended their lives with one quick order to the guards. He didn't, but he did take a moment to do what comes so naturally to guys when they interact with other guys: he messed with their heads. You can read the story in Genesis 42–45, but suffice it to say that Joseph's brothers experienced enough anxiety to get their attention and remind them of how horribly they had acted toward him.

The moment passed, and in the end Joseph showed his brothers compassion and mercy. He gave them food to care for their families. He shared a great meal with them and eventually resettled the whole clan in Egypt, where they lived under his care.

Joseph was a steward of God. He defied the gravity of circumstance and the temptations of the cultures in which he had been raised. He did not accept the advances of Potiphar's wife. He did not punish the brothers who had enslaved him. He gave to his family when they were in need and he had wealth and power. He was faithful to God whether he was living in a prison cell or in the pharaoh's villa.

By accepting the identity of a steward, Joseph learned to honor God in the way he spent his time, abilities, talents, and resources. The great accomplishment of Joseph's life was not the job he held in Egypt but the generous character he developed under harsh circumstances. Serving God and others, Joseph emerged as a man who generously saved rather than destroyed.

THE PATH TO STEWARDSHIP

Sometimes when we talk about stewardship, it sounds like God is after our money. The story of Joseph shows us that God is out for something much more valuable—that we give our lives to the work of God's kingdom. When Joseph rose above his circumstances to become a steward, he broke a long cycle of dysfunctional competition and contempt, turning enemies back into family.

The key to being a steward is offering our lives to God with joy so that we can mature and be transformed over time. This is why generosity is a gravity-defying act. The gravity of this world makes it seem impossible to display the devotion and sacrifice generosity to God requires while at the same time experiencing joy. As we grow in our identity as stewards, we will increasingly make sacrifices to be generous with our time, character, and money in ways that will result in joy instead of resentment.

Our progression to joyous stewardship was described by Francis de Sales, a sixteenth-century Catholic priest and bishop. De Sales wrote that our initial experience of God occurs when our soul first experiences grace. In that moment, grace "adorns our souls" and makes us pleasing to God. De Sales compared people at this initial state of grace to an ostrich. An ostrich can run but cannot fly. Similarly, if a person receives God's love and grace but does not have the devotion to respond in some way to God, the person cannot fly. Such people, wanting to get something from God but not willing to give of themselves in return, can't break the gravity of this world even for a moment, and therefore they spend their time desperately looking for new ways to receive God's love and mercy.

De Sales went on to say there is another step in the spiritual life. It occurs when a person responds to God's grace through occasional acts of goodness or charity. At this stage there is a response, but the acts of goodness are short-lived. Such people, said de Sales, are like chickens. Chickens can fly, but always in a limited and clumsy way. Chickens spend the vast majority of their time on the ground. They can only break free from gravity for a short time before they return to earth. As a result, their lives are spent in a very limited space. De Sales states:

> In like manner, sinners in no way fly up towards God, but make their whole course here upon the earth and for the earth. Good people who have not as yet attained to devotion fly toward God by their good works but do so infrequently, slowly and awkwardly.[1]

This means that my problem in my early married life was that I acted like a big chicken! Devotion, according to de Sales, is the key to freedom and joy in the Christian life. People who are fully devoted to God fly like the birds of the air. Taking flight as naturally as eagles, doves, or swallows, such people receive God's grace and become dedicated to God with their whole lives. They long to serve God with all they have: their ability, time, strength, and resources. Such people are generous for God because they both recognize and celebrate God's generosity to them. According to de Sales, there is a powerful outcome in a life devoted to Christ: "Devout souls ascend to him frequently, promptly and with lofty flights. In short, devotion is simply that spiritual agility and vivacity by which charity works in us or by aid of which we work quickly and lovingly."[2]

One reason that many people never move from ostrich to eagle is that the increased devotion required for each new stage feels too much like sacrifice. Here, it's important for us to acknowledge that sacrifice is sacrifice. Though generosity may be a path to deeper joy and freedom, it does require us to part with things we may hold dear and offer up things we would rather use for other purposes.

This is why the practice of tithing can be so difficult for married couples who are in two different places regarding stewardship. For one partner, giving money to a church or nonprofit is an act of commitment to God's work in the community, based on an awareness of all God has done in their lives. To the other partner, giving is a painful loss of money that could have been enjoyed in the present or saved for the future. While one spouse freely invests money in something they believe in, the other mourns what they could have enjoyed if the money was still theirs. Even though both may love Jesus and go to church, they live in a divided house because of the varying degree of financial gravity each one experiences.

We cannot blame Jesus for such a predicament in our personal lives or relationships. Jesus told us that sacrifice would be part of what it means to follow him. The author of the Gospel of Matthew records Jesus' statement:

> "Those who don't pick up their crosses and follow me aren't worthy of me. Those who find their lives will lose them, and those who lose their lives because of me will find them."
>
> (Matthew 10:38-39)

When a similar quotation appears in the Gospel of Luke, it is stated even more strongly: "All who want to come after me must say no to themselves, take up their cross daily, and follow me" (Luke 9:23).

There may be passages in the Bible that are unclear to modern readers, but these passages are not among them. Here Jesus puts us on notice that sacrifice is a part of the package. The beautiful cross that today adorns the sanctuary or hangs from a necklace had only one purpose in Jesus' time. It was a cruel instrument of death, a warning that the Romans were in control and were not to be defied.

Jesus' life ended on a cross. This was the greatest act of generosity, fulfilling what Jesus had told his disciples earlier: "No one has greater love than to give up one's life for one's friends" (John 15:13). When Jesus' followers later recorded his statement that they would have to pick up their crosses daily, they knew that sacrifice was going to be involved.

Thankfully, the vast majority of Christians in the United States will never know the type of sacrifice Jesus experienced. And yet, based on the statistics we discussed previously about giving by Christians, even a modest level of sacrifice seems for many Christians to be too painful a cross to bear. By contrast, the Christians who do accept the challenge and make the sacrifice find that their appreciation of God's love and grace more than compensates for any loss they experience.

Such appreciation is unrelated to income level; it can be experienced in scarcity as easily as in plenitude. Glen James, a homeless Boston man, found a backpack outside a shopping mall containing $42,000 in cash and traveler's checks, along with the passport of a Chinese student who mistakenly left it behind. Rather than keep it, James flagged down a police car so the money could be returned to its rightful owner. James, who lives in a homeless shelter and occasionally panhandles for change to wash his clothes, was honored for his honesty. When thanked at a ceremony by Boston Police Commissioner Edward Davis, James replied, "Even if I were desperate for money, I would not have kept even a penny of the money I found. I am extremely religious—God has always very well looked after me."[3]

Glen James defied financial gravity. Money and possessions had no power over him, even when he lived daily in need of life's essentials. This former file clerk, who had been homeless five years when he found the bag of money, had a clear vision about the way he would live his life, even in times of financial hardship. His simple desire to honor God defined the way he lived. He was honest and understood what was his and what belonged to others. Glen James demonstrated empathy and compassion to the student who had left his bag behind. The decision to return the bag was a sacrifice that James made freely and joyfully, in acknowledgment of all that God had done for him.

DEFYING GRAVITY

If you would like to break free from the culture of more and experience generosity with joy, I encourage you first to consider the ongoing impact of financial gravity in our world.

Patricia Greenfield has done research on families in Chiapas, Mexico, for over forty years. Though many of the families were experiencing subsistence poverty when she began, they grew in their financial security, and Greenfield discovered an important correlation. The more wealth people enjoyed, the more individualistic and self-oriented they became. Community and even family ties frayed and weakened. Caring for family members and neighbors became less important over time.

Greenfield wondered if the same correlation would hold true on a more general basis. She analyzed more than one million books published in the United States between 1800 and 2000, a time period when the US economy grew to become the largest and most productive in the world.

> "The frequency of the word 'get' went up, and the frequency of the word 'give' went down," she said. The words Americans used to describe themselves changed, too. "Words that would show an individualistic orientation became more frequent. Examples of those words were 'individual,' 'self,' 'unique,'" she said. "Words that would represent a more communal or more family orientation went down in frequency. Some examples of those words are 'give,' 'obliged,' 'belong.'"[4]

Greenfield's research pushes us to consider who we become when we allow the force of financial gravity to go unabated. The practices of generosity allow us to be free to care for family and address the needs of our neighbor. They enable us to do good in our church so that the church can do good in our community. Generosity is a reminder that if we are God's stewards, the focus of life is no longer on what brings us quick satisfaction or on which comforts serve to cushion our existence. Through generosity, we break free of a good life so we can find a great one.

But it's not easy. Financial gravity is relentless. Every week, I get e-mails from a company that sells goods for a reduced price. I've attempted to unsubscribe from these e-mails on a few occasions, but somehow they always come back. One day I looked carefully at what I could purchase. They were offering dome-shaped NFL team cups. I pictured a group of friends gathered around a TV for a football game. I imagined everyone holding their matching NFL cups, rooting on their team. That could be good. Those cups could be used weekly during football season before they were banished to the back of a cabinet somewhere.

That same day I saw photos of children who formerly lived at the Child Rescue Centre (CRC), a home that our church supports for children who are victims of child trafficking and child labor in Sierra Leone, Africa. These were beautiful photos of young men and women who were graduating college and vocational school and were ready to live independent, adult lives. I thought about all the donations that made it happen. Many people invested amounts, small and large, in these young adults when they were children. That money paid for their food, clothing, and education. It paid salaries of the staff who raised and supported them.

Some of the donors, besides contributing money, traveled to Sierra Leone to teach, tutor, and care for these young people. One couple became so generously committed to the CRC that they spent almost an entire year on the two-acre campus during the Ebola crisis of 2014–15, helping maintain heath protocols that kept the children free from this deadly infection. It was an amazingly generous act.

There's nothing wrong with an NFL dome cup. It can be good. But I promise you this: Long after you've recycled your NFL cups, gifts like those given to the CRC and other great causes in the world will still be doing good. You don't have to go to Africa to find those causes. The possibilities are all around you. They are in your church, your neighborhood, your community. Every time you are generous with your time, talent, or treasure, you have invested in something that is truly great.

All of us can defy gravity. It doesn't take lots of money. It does take time. It takes sacrifice. It takes a shift in our view of the world. We must learn to see our lives as belonging to God and trust that God will direct our lives in a generous way that will bring us joy and significance.

God longs for us to experience a life in Christ that will make us generous in all ways, with our kindness, compassion, and love as evidenced in the use of our time and money. Such a life enables us to break free of the world's gravity and enjoy the pull of God's kingdom so that the Spirit of God will be evident in our own.

NOTES

CHAPTER ONE

1   Radio Lab, "Is There an Edge to the Heavens?" accessed on Jan. 29, 2016, http://www.radiolab.org/story/187718-edge-heavens/; Edward Dolnick, *The Clockwork Universe: Isaac Newton, the Royal Society, and the Birth of the Modern World* (New York: Harper, 2013).

2   NASA, Sandra Magnus, *"Food and Cooking in Space, Part 2,"* accessed on January 29, 2016, http://www.nasa.gov/mission_pages/station/expeditions/expedition18/journal_sandra_magnus_7.html.

3   Dallas Willard, *The Divine Conspiracy: Rediscovering Our Hidden Life in God* (New York: Harper, 1998), 21.

4   Ibid., 27.

CHAPTER TWO

1   Christian Smith and Hillary Davidson, *The Paradox of Generosity: Giving We Receive, Grasping We Lose* (Oxford: Oxford University Press, 2014), 3–4.

2   Lois Smith Brady, "Chee-Yun Kim and Eugene Kim," *New York Times* (Aug. 24, 1997), http://www.nytimes.com/1997/08/24/style/chee-yun-kim-and-eugene-kim.html. Accessed 2-27-2016.

3   "World-renowned violinist plans instrument that's back from the grave," http://fox2now.com/2014/10/19/world-renowned-violinist-plays-instrument-thats-back-from-the-grave/. Accessed 2-27-2016.

4   Smith and Davidson, *The Paradox of Generosity*, 99.

5   Ibid., 103.

6   Ibid., 99.

7   Christian Smith, Michael O. Emerson, and Patricia Snell, *Passing the Plate: Why Americans Don't Give Away More Money* (Oxford: Oxford University Press, 2008), 29, 38.

8   Ibid., 34, 36–37.

9   Smith, *The Paradox of Generosity*, 99.

CHAPTER THREE

1   Tim Brady, "The Orteig Prize," Journal of *Aviation/Aerospace* Education & Research 12, no. 9 (Fall 2002), 48–49.

2   Ibid.

3   Ibid., 55.

4   Ibid., 51–52.

5   Charles Lindbergh, *The Spirit of St. Louis* (New York: Charles Scribner's and Sons, 1953), 17.

6   Brady, "The Orteig Prize," 58.

7   Charles Lindbergh, an American Aviator, "Charles Lindbergh Biography," accessed on Jan. 29, 2016, http://www.charleslindbergh.com/history/.

8   Thomas Stanley and William Danko, *The Millionaire Next Door: The Surprising Secrets of America's Wealthy* (New York: Taylor Trade Publishing, 2010).

9 NASA, "Space Debris and Human Spacecraft," September 26, 2013, http://www.nasa.gov/mission_pages/station/news/orbital_debris .html.

10 Josh Sanburn, "The Joy of Less," *TIME*, Mar. 23, 2015, 49.

11 "Shoe shiner donates $200K in tips to children in need." WTAE.COM ABC Action News Pittsburgh, retrieved Sept. 7, 2015.

12 Ashley Bleimes, "Institute recognizes 13 caring Americans of all ages," *USA TODAY*, Oct. 16, 2006, http://usatoday30.usatoday.com /news/nation/2006-10-16-caring-awards_x.htm.

CHAPTER FOUR

1 Saint Francis de Sales, *Introduction to the Devout Life*, translated by John K. Ryan (1972; New York: Image Books, 2003), 28.

2 Ibid., 28–29.

3 Peter Schworm, "Police Honor Homeless Man's Good Deed," *Boston Globe*, Sep. 16, 2013, https://www.bostonglobe.com/metro/2013/09/16 /glen-james-homeless-man-who-returned-bag-cash-honored-boston -police/yUZjfKiELlXDURjhQwQ23O/story.html.

4 Shankar Vedantam, "As we become richer, do we become stingier?" *Hidden Brain*, Nashville Public Radio, Sep. 3, 2007, http://www .npr.org/2013/09/03/218627288/why-being-wealthy-doesnt -lead-to-more-giving.

ACKNOWLEDGMENTS

Defying Gravity arose out of conversations with my wife, Karen. Her observations about the value of simplicity and the joy of generosity have been formative to my life. My colleagues at Floris United Methodist Church—Pam Piester, Barbara Miner, Tim Ward, Cynthia Lopynski, Bill Gray, and Jake McGlothin—worked together to plan and execute worship services, events, and related materials that made this an experience our congregation found meaningful. Charlie Kendall and Justin Lucas at Moon Bounce Media brought their usual creativity, knowledge, and unwillingness to settle for good when better is only a few takes away.

Pam Borland, my administrative assistant, kindly read and edited materials and manuscripts. The Ministry Resources team at Abingdon Press acted as conversation partners in developing the ideas and are deeply appreciated. My family provided a great sounding board for ideas and observations.

Finally, I am grateful to the members of Floris UMC, who have been kind enough to talk with me about their call to be Christian stewards and about the way generosity has transformed their lives. The insights they've shared have confirmed the wisdom of the Bible and the calling of Christ to seek first the kingdom of God and its righteousness.

ABOUT THE AUTHOR

Tom Berlin is Senior Pastor of Floris United Methodist Church in Herndon, Virginia. He is a graduate of Virginia Tech and Candler School of Theology at Emory University. Tom is author of *Defying Gravity: Break Free from the Culture of More*; *6 Decisions That Will Change Your Life*; *6 Things We Should Know About God*; and *6 Ways We Encounter God*. He is coauthor (with Lovett H. Weems, Jr.) of *Bearing Fruit: Ministry with Real Results*; *Overflow: Increase Worship Attendance and Bear More Fruit*; and *High Yield: Seven Disciplines of the Fruitful Leader*.